SUPERNATURAL MANIFESTATIONS IN THE CHURCH

DEAL WITH THE DEVIL

JOSEPH SCHELLENBERG, D.C.C.

WESTBOW PRESS
A DIVISION OF THOMAS NELSON
& ZONDERVAN

Copyright © 2014 Joseph Schellenberg, D.C.C.

All rights reserved. No part of this book may be used or reproduced by any means, graphic, electronic, or mechanical, including photocopying, recording, taping or by any information storage retrieval system without the written permission of the publisher except in the case of brief quotations embodied in critical articles and reviews.

Scripture taken from the King James Version of the Bible.

Scripture quotations taken from the Holy Bible, New Living Translation, copyright 1996, 2004. Used by permission of Tyndale House Publishers, Inc., Wheaton, Illinois 60189. All rights reserved.

WestBow Press books may be ordered through booksellers or by contacting:

WestBow Press
A Division of Thomas Nelson & Zondervan
1663 Liberty Drive
Bloomington, IN 47403
www.westbowpress.com
1 (866) 928-1240

Because of the dynamic nature of the Internet, any web addresses or links contained in this book may have changed since publication and may no longer be valid. The views expressed in this work are solely those of the author and do not necessarily reflect the views of the publisher, and the publisher hereby disclaims any responsibility for them.

Any people depicted in stock imagery provided by Thinkstock are models, and such images are being used for illustrative purposes only. Certain stock imagery © Thinkstock.

ISBN: 978-1-4908-4004-8 (sc)
ISBN: 978-1-4908-4003-1 (hc)
ISBN: 978-1-4908-4005-5 (e)

Library of Congress Control Number: 2014910493

Printed in the United States of America.

WestBow Press rev. date: 06/06/2014

ACKNOWLEDGMENTS

My family who live to ascribe meaningful authorship to my life.

Artistry: Dean Foster Cartoons and Illustrations
(see *website deanfostercartoons.com*)

CONTENTS

Introduction xv
A Ball of Fire.. xv
The Human Factor xvi

Chapter 1: Let Thy Work Appear 1

Chapter 2: Speaking in Tongues? Never! 8
The Work and Person of the Holy Spirit 9

**Chapter 3: Twenty-One (Plus One) Gifts of the
Spirit for the Church** 13
Administration 14
Operations 14
Manifestations 15
Miracles: Gifts of Healing 16
Utterance Gifts 17
Tongues and Interpretation 19

Chapter 4: Born to Be Broken, Broken to Bring Healing 20
Eight Kinds of Tongues 22
Power and Void Teaching 27

Chapter 5: Manifestation in Relation to Hunger for God 29
Angels Tinkling the Piano Keys 29
Glory and Gifting 30
Engagement with the Enemy..31

Chapter 6: Other Manifestations in Spiritual Intercession.... 36
Groaning in the Spirit 37
Travailing in the Spirit 38
Roaring in the Spirit 38
Militant Tongues...40
Spiritual Barking...40
Counterfeit Spiritual Experiences 42

Chapter 7: In the Mud Room..45
Manifestations at the Toronto Blessing......................................47
Bizarre Spiritual Manifestations 49
Decently and in Order 50
Holy Laughter...51

Chapter 8: Prayer and the Sovereignty of God 53
The Plane Roared Back up into the Sky 53
Tongues: A Tangible Link for the Supernatural 54
Praying Mysteries 55
God Is Only as Sovereign as His Word......................................57
Authority in Two Realms?..58
Can Jesus Pray for Us in Heaven?..59

Chapter 9: Militant Prayer: Deliver Us from Evil 65
Big Demons on the Roof...65
The Blast of His Nostrils...65
He Grabbed His Chest and Fell to the Floor.............................66

Is Satan to Be Feared? 66
All Called to Prayer, Not All Called to the Office of Prayer 68

**Chapter 10: Other Manifestations, Outpourings,
and the Voice of the Lord** 70
Spiritual Shaking 70
How Does an Outpouring such as the Toronto Blessing Begin? 72
A Direct Tongue to Deal with the Devil 73
The Voice of the Lord 74

**Chapter 11: One Cannot Lead Where One Has
Never Gone** 78

Chapter 12: Music and Worship in the Modern World 81
Musical Snoring and Croaking 81
The Key Is the Anointing 83
Supernatural Spiritual Songs 86
Aboriginal Cultures More Accepting of Spiritual Experiences 86
Be Renewed in the Spirit of Your Mind 87

Chapter 13: The Roar of the Lord 90
Roaring with Big Ushers 90
Preservice Intercession 91

**Chapter 14: The Church and One's Personal
Devotion to God** 94
Adam and Eve 94
The Church: A Verbal Experience 95
Dry Sermons 96

Chapter 15: Prayer with the Understanding 98
After This Manner Pray Ye 98

Chapter 16: Spiritual Transference 102
Physical Gestures Empowered against the Enemy 103
Laying on of Hands 104
Anointing with Oil: Lifting up Holy Hands 105
Prayer and Declaration 106
Baby Talk 106
Territorial Churches 108
Being Spiritual in a Physical World 108

Chapter 17: A Demon's Tongue? Possible Explanations 109
My Prayer Shop 110
The Ball of Fire 110
The Law of Parsimony 111
Facts v. Truth: Diseases Are Caused by Germs 113

Chapter 18: The Healing Ministry of Jesus 116
An Example of Healing 116
The Leper 118
The Centurion's Servant 118
The Woman with the Issue of Blood 118
Jairus's Daughter 118
The Nobleman's Son 119
Peter's Mother-in-Law 119
On Faith 119

Chapter 19: Ten Kinds of Prayer 121
The Prayer with Other Tongues (1 Corinthians 14:18) 122
The Prayer of Consecration and Dedication (Mark 14:36) 122

The Prayer of Agreement 122
The Prayer of Fellowship 123
The Prayer of Intercession 123
The Prayer of Faith 124
The Prayer of Commitment 124
Binding and Loosing 125
Commanding Power 125
The Prayer of Praise, Thanksgiving, and Worship 126

Chapter 20: Daily Prayer: Deliver Us from evil 129
If We Forget to Pray, We Will Have More Trouble 129
If We Forget to Pray, We May Be Sinning 129
Intercession: A Special Gift? 130
Prayer Is Our Way of Receiving God's Gifts as well as His Goodness 132

Chapter 21: Various Forms of Prayer 134
Crying unto the Lord 134
Dialogue 135
Corporate Prayer 135
Prayer Posture 136
Times and Places of Prayer 137

Chapter 22: Help in Prevailing Prayer 138
Fasting 138
Heartfelt Earnestness 139
Keeping a Journal 139

Chapter 23: A Treasure without a Measure 141
Wine Tasting or Just a Sip Will Do 141
For Us and/or Others 142

Oil and Wine 143
A Real Gusher! 144
Wine, Worship, and Soaking in His Presence 145

Chapter 24: Special Miracles, Prophetic Dreams, and Levels of Anointing 148
Prophetic Dreams 150
Personal Level of Anointing 151
Anointed Ministry Gifts 151
The Corporate Anointing 151

Chapter 25: Special Tactical Squad 154
Diversity of Tongues in Dealing with the Devil 154
Diabolos-Evil Schemer 155
Huddles and Game Play 156
Row, Row, Row Your Boat! 156

Chapter 26: Free Will: Man v. God… and the Devil 158
God's Word Is Supernatural 160
Putting a Demand on God's Word 161

Chapter 27: Praying Mysteries 163
The Mysteries of God 163
Great Is the Mystery of Godliness 164

Chapter 28: Deal with the Devil 166
Autopilot? 166
Anointing Released through Gaze and Command 167

Chapter 29: Biblical Structure 169

Chapter 30: Summary, Signs, and Symptoms.......................171
Supernatural Burning..171
Supernatural Tranquility...172
Deep Emotional Release..173
The Spirit without Measure..173

INTRODUCTION

A Ball of Fire

Years ago when I was a teenager and was in my bedroom at night, I remember what appeared to be a large ball of fire rolling slowly past my bedroom window. Our house was an old house, and it had lots of tall windows.

Moments later two boys from town who were walking by our house at night on their way to the town skating rink were excitedly knocking at our door. They said, "We just saw a big ball of fire roll around your house!"

I give a response to this strange event later on in chapters on subjective experiences, but it raises a question. Does a physical phenomenon always have a rational explanation, or are there intangible spiritual forces at work behind the scenes?

It is my desire to bring emphasis and restoration to a significant aspect of the supernatural. We are a people whose identity is found in relationship to a supernatural God who has made all things for Himself. We must reacquaint ourselves with the operations of this God, whom the Bible declares as having no beginning and no ending, who always was and who always will be (see Revelation 1:8). Our security is not in that which has a beginning or an ending. Our lives must be complete in Him.

This is why it is not spiritual manifestations we are seeking but God. God is not boring. He made us, and He has made this most intricately woven place called the universe. He does not expect us to provide or look after ourselves physically or spiritually. We were made by Him, for Him, and through Him. We need God—body, soul, and spirit. Because He desires to partner with us in His covenant, He has given us a share and responsibility in the creative process.

This most certainly involves an extraordinary, sometimes irrational link to reality. Most times just when we've written out the parameters of our faith experiences, God takes them and makes papier–mâché out of them. It is our inclination then to mold them into figurines and paint them up to resemble something that bears an image to our physical modes, something we can manage within the confines of our frame of reference.

The apostle Paul inferred that we have made the Word of God of "none effect" through our traditions. It is the fear of moving out of our limited spectrum of experience and comfort zone that keeps us from moving into the supernatural.

Rationale, great minds and the desire to experience God on our terms keeps us from entering into greater depths of revelation. We say, "This is the box, God. Show up." Instead God says, "You don't have room enough to contain the blessing that I want to pour out on you!"

The Human Factor

God desires to show Himself as strong in the small things as well as the great. This is where the flexibility of being a functional human in the physical universe and being an empowered carrier of the gospel must be anatomical in structure. They must function together.

The apostle Paul gave some practical advice. People were getting caught up in the things of the spirit but forgot that along with what God was doing in and through the church, they had a physical existence. Paul gave advice to the Thessaloninans, to work with their own hands, and to live a quiet and peaceable life. Physical things were meant to be enjoyed. He might say, "Buy a new truck," if you like, but you need to work for it so that it is really yours to enjoy!

The human element requires us to get out of bed, shower, eat, and sleep. We need people to care for, and we need to be cared for on an emotional level. What God requires is for us to do our part. We present ourselves physically ready, doing whatever is within our power, and we expect Him to do His part.

When God does not move, we need to begin to rehearse and commend His Word to ourselves in prayer and confession. We stir ourselves up to receive the Word, and then God comes in. There is always something or someone who holds a key to every great demonstration of God's power.

A great artist may have excellent inspiration, but he must have some skill with a brush or an instrument. We do our part and present ourselves ready. Then God says, "Here is the creative genius. You be the instrument that facilitates its' release into the earth."

Whether it is great music, storytelling, or painting, we must have a finely tuned instrument to release the greatness of the inspiration.

This is present in every facet of the arts. We need some amount of skill with something. Even developing hand-eye coordination is essential in running critical machinery. Experts get the best jobs.

When God wants to show Himself as strong, He may look for leaders who already possess a spirit of excellence. It is character that is needed more than skills, but we need skilled individuals to be relevant in a physical world.

When I came to work this morning, I had no appointments, but I know that I am an essential part of God's creation. I am loved and known by Him, whether others find me significant or not. The discipline required to be faithful when no one is calling upon you is learned. We need to prepare the way for the Lord to come in and to pray the Lord's Prayer every morning even when things look worse today than they did yesterday.

Greatness is not arrived at in a day. "David went on and grew great, and God was with him" (1 Samuel 5:10). We look at persons who have a history of making good decisions. They are not necessarily more clever than the rest of us.

I had a friend who would just stop in the middle of an event and pray. She would say, "I just want to be quiet for a while now." Then she would pray quietly. Then everything would be normal again.

God does want us to enter into His rest. He has green pastures where He is restoring our souls. Even if we are called to a particularly tough kind of life, God still gives us the stamina to push things through. Some people are in continual warfare. Some of their conflicts may be self-sabotage where they do not stop and enter into the rest of God or wait for leading.

Some leaders may be hardened for the ministry and ready to fight for what is not the popular message of the day. In that sense hardness is a scriptural characteristic for leadership (see 2 Timothy 2:3). Leadership requires a certain amount of tenacity. One will need to engage the same intensity in finding places of rest. The human factor cannot be ignored.

A heart of understanding maintains a good sense of what we need on a personal level. We need to stop and ask God for it. We are not asking enough. James 4:2 says, "You are missing out because you are not asking." The supernatural must accompany the natural. We cannot expect to burn up for God without experiencing burnout on a personal level.

The supernatural has a natural realm. But it cannot be defined by the natural. It is supernatural. What then defines the manifestation of the supernatural in the church?

We must realize that God hasn't left us without a frame of reference. Our experience must be in correlation to His Word. Taking our experience and augmenting it with scripture usually results in the real truth being a bit skewed. We need to implement supportive arguments from the Word that will not only stand on their own text but have parallel affirmations from an exegetical standpoint.

Expressions of form and experience are not always specifically addressed in scripture. An example comes from worship. Interpretation and form have a subjective element left to the conjecture of the participants. How one worships, whether with hymnbooks, choruses, or overhead projection with music, are nonessentials when it comes to substance and doctrine.

We cannot build on modes, but expression (worship for instance) has form and structure. The supernatural may accompany a particular form, but form doesn't sanction or produce an entitlement.

The supernatural is evident and recorded throughout the Bible. How we perceive it is always viewed through the lens of our experience. At times we may need to reconstruct of the ideals we hold to (see Jeremiah 1:10).

What is our responsibility in relation to the Great Commission? If it is by God's choosing that we are saved, then why go out and evangelize? I believe there is an element of believing that is essential to God releasing His power.

This holds the same for receiving salvation or appropriating His promises. The fact that the "just shall live by faith" has more implications than mere repentance. We must go on in believing to greater levels of faith for the greater works that Jesus spoke of in John 14:12.

From the beginning of time God has given man huge responsibility for what happens on the earth. The very first command God gave man (and woman) was to have dominion. We are to be man, and He is to be God. With instructions from God, I have an uncompromising and divine enablement.

We know it is not God's will that any should perish. How can we then be so complacent? God is credited with the atrocities of the Devil when we have been given the power and authority to deal with him ourselves.

We search for answers, putting together strange inequalities between the sovereignty of God and the one who allows evil and is at the same time good.

We adopt a subtle doctrinal error when we say, "In the sovereignty of God, He does what He wills." We in natural North America are living the good life and do not see that the supernatural is absolutely essential in making an impact on this world.

Tongues are a tangible link of the natural to the supernatural. In the "praying more than ye all" (1 Corinthians 4:18) tongue that Paul prayed in, he kept a faith supply and residue of the anointing ready as the needs in his life warranted it. I believe the level of revelation he received in writing half the New Testament was related to this dimension of his prayer language. Other types of utterances were for other kinds of manifestations. We need them all.

Specifically we need to have a tongue in intercession that deals with the Devil on a corporate level. This means corporate intercession. This rarely occurs because of the rigidity with which pastors rule their churches. The level of evangelical thrust in some churches is relegated to the handing out of "big daddy" tracts on the street.

Some churches have embarked on what they call "prophetic evangelism." This is prayer for the purpose of prophetic insight and leading on whom they are to talk to. For instance, after they pray together, they receive a spiritual impression to go out into the mall and approach someone wearing a green jacket. They go to that person and ask him or her if he or she needs prayer for something.

This is a more targeted approach, accessing the gifts of the Spirit but still not entering in to the depths of what God desires to accomplish in the church.

The last admonition from the pulpit Sunday morning might typically be "to go out and be the church." God didn't say that we should go out and be the church without the glory being first poured into the church. It is then that the church will have an effect. People will come from every part of the world to see what is happening.

When the glory begins to manifest in the church, signs and wonders will bring in every reporter from every tabloid in the country. Every cable network will want a part of it. God knows how to get the attention. We don't need to do it for Him. When we begin to make a holy atmosphere for His presence, the king of glory will come in. Psalm 24:7 says, "Lift up your heads, O ye gates, and be ye lift up ye heavenly doors, and the King of Glory shall come in." Holy and revered is His name.

We have lost serving God with reverence and godly fear. God does not ask us to bear up under the weight and burden of millions of souls perishing. We must accept responsibility for the glory. God will bring in the souls if we take care of His glory.

God's desire is to pour out His glory in a greater measure than He did in Solomon's temple. It was there that "the priests could not enter in to minister," for the glory had filled the temple. It is there that with creative genius and emphasis, Asaph made all the musical instruments for David's worship team.

Musical expression is like wind and fragrance. It moves as a wand that waves and woos one's spirit into the presence of God. We must begin to feel and crave the tangible atmosphere of His presence.

I was amazed at how the world took up the "end of the world" message of 2011 in the movies and on secular media. It is because the Holy Spirit has been poured out upon all flesh. People are hungering for Him and seeking to fill the vacuum. They are seeking the Holy Spirit in supernatural power. We must have relevant answers and a manifestation of His glory to give them.

The experiences I have related are real and vital, but they are my experiences. Everyone has a testimony. That is the vitality of the Christian life.

I believe God wants us to go deeper in revelation of the supernatural, and in areas of the utterance gifts. Manifestations are the third grouping of the twenty-one gifts of the Holy Spirit in the release of revelation, power, and utterance. These are essential in releasing the supernatural. We can only go so far with our understanding.

You may have a doctorate in theological studies, recite scripture in your sleep, and yet have an incredible ineptitude in spiritual warfare. Apart from the Spirit of God giving revelation and utterance, we are merely tinkling jars or brass cymbals. Our words just salve our egos.

In this manuscript I give weight to the whole area of tongues. This is vital both in building up ourselves in our spirit man as well as engaging the Enemy in spiritual warfare. I am appalled at the weakness of ministers of God. They may have eloquence, but they are emaciated and malnourished in their spirit man.

This is also to give understanding to the realm of spiritual warfare in the influence and effect we have in building the kingdom of God. Like Nehemiah, we build with a trowel in one hand and a sword in the other. It is the Spirit of God that partners with us in engaging the Devil through militant tongues. When we pray in tongues like Paul, we will begin to release the Word like a hammer and the Spirit of God like a sword. It is then that we will break and pierce through the hardest ground the Enemy has strategically held.

Taking a region must involve a breaker anointing, where a few intercessors go in to establish a stronghold. Strong preaching, declaration and resources must follow. It is only by the Spirit of God that we topple territorial despots. It is only the Spirit of God that can enforce the relinquishing and release of their tyrannical reign over a region. Jesus said, "If I with the finger of God (the Holy Spirit) cast out devils, no doubt the kingdom of God is come unto you" (Luke 12:20). If Jesus needed the Holy Spirit, whom He possessed without measure, how much more do we need to access the gifts He has placed within the body? We are the church, and together we possess the same measure; however, we must make sure that each part is functioning.

On what basis do we demand Satan relinquish his right? It is on the finished work of the cross and the blood of an everlasting covenant on which a bastion and bulwark can be established for the kingdom of God. It is from there that the kingdom of God can execute its sphere of operations.

It is in that place of rest that others can come in out from the darkness and oppression of Satan. It is in that place where others can come and rest until they are restored to the kingdom. We have the power, but we must execute the authority. Exercising this authority involves engaging the Enemy through militant tongues.

CHAPTER 1

LET THY WORK APPEAR

An Anglican minister died and went to heaven. St. Peter took him through the pearly gates and down a long corridor with golden paving stones. As they came around the corner, St. Peter whispered to the Anglican minister, "Shhh… we must be quiet here. This is the section where the Mennonites[1] are, and they think they are the only ones here!"

This type of sectarian thinking prevails in most denominations. We have difficulty moving into any realm that takes us outside the parameters of our experience.

Experience may perceive cognition and rationale as a wonderful thing in a rational universe. Conversely seeing the earth as part of a larger universe invites the supernatural in for explanation. It may be that God is using foolishness and absurdity to shake up religious ideology and destroy the lofty wisdom of man.

It is vital to bring back the God of the Bible. It is only then that we understand supernatural manifestations. Beginning with the study of origins, we see the supernatural displayed, as the Holy Spirit hovered over the face of the deep (see Genesis 1:2). There was

---

[1] With a name like Schellenberg, do you think…?! I am of Mennonite heritage.

a period of gestation when form, invention, and intervention were being accomplished in secret.

The word *ruach*[2] is one of the Hebrew translations for Holy Spirit. Here the words *mind, breath, understanding,* and *wind* characterize the reforming of the earth. One of the characteristics for Spirit is displayed in the Hebrew word *neshamah*,[3] which indicates "a blast." Psalm 18:15–17 says, "Then the channels of water were seen, and the foundations of the world were discovered. At thy rebuke, O Lord, at the blast of thy nostrils. He sent from above, he took me, he drew me out of many waters, He delivered me from my strong enemy."

These words characterize elements of the spirit that I feel are still involved in how God delivers us from the power of evil. The Word operates in conjunction with the Spirit. At the appointed (paga)[4] time there is a meeting place, and the work of God appears.

Psalm 104 says that God "casts forth His lightning bolts." This is a picture of the manifestation of how something appears at the right time and hits the mark when the Word is spoken over it. Genesis 1:4 illustrates this. "Let there be light, and there was light."

Out of the depths and in the womb of God, the Spirit of God begins to work. The manifestation of it appears only after the Spirit has travailed in birth. Paul spoke of this ministry in the spirit, where God used him to "travail in birth" until Christ could be formed in them.

The pattern in Romans 8:26–28 indicates that God does not randomly work apart from the intercession of the Spirit. It is only

---

[2] *Young's Analytical Concordance to the Bible,* p. 41 Index Lexicon to the Old Testament.

[3] *Young's Analytical Concordance to the Bible,* p. 32 Index Lexicon to the Old Testament.

[4] Romans 8:26 to light upon, (paga) to meet together; to make intercession, 6293 Greek Lexicon, *Strongs Concordance.*

as the Spirit intercedes for us with inarticulate speech or expressions that baffle human language and reason that the will and purpose of God begins to take form and all things work together for good.

The operation of the Holy Spirit is interwoven with the spirit of man and subject to the ability of that union to bring the will of God into the earth. As Christ dwells in us by faith, we become a work of God in process.

We are His workmanship, created in Christ Jesus unto good works, foreordained that we should walk in them. Even as the Spirit of God moved upon the earth, so He is moving to bring forth a people who will partner with Him in enforcing His conquest over Satan.

We are to have dominion over everything that is made in the earth (Genesis 1:26). Jesus conquered the flesh, the world, hell, and the grave. He gives the power but has delegated the authority to us.

In Matthew 28:18, Jesus said, "All power is given unto me both in heaven and in earth; Go ye therefore." He then commissions His disciples to that end, enduing and empowering them for the making of disciples and the preaching of the gospel (Acts 1:8).

Mark 16:18 adds the element of transmitting power through the laying on of hands for healing the sick. He makes a promise to those who believe to protect them from snakes, scorpions, poison, or any other harmful elements that might be devised against them.

Only Jesus can really love the people of this earth through us. Only Jesus can bring an end to the reign and terror of Satan through the church, His body.

He has done His part. It is now up to us to implement and put an end to the infiltration of the Enemy. We have the Word, which is the sword of the Spirit, but we are missing the full revelation of the Spirit. How we receive more of Him is multifaceted.

Joseph Schellenberg, D.C.C.

Let Thy Work Appear

> Let thy work appear unto thy servants, and thy glory unto their children.
> —Psalm 90:16

God desires to reveal Himself to the children of men. We have limited Him with our experiential knowledge. It is like the gifted composers of other eras, such as Bach, Handel, and Mozart, or an artist like Michelangelo. There is a release of something wonderful from heaven for a particular purpose and demonstration. It is the heavenly gift and inspiration that accompanies the work and skill of the composer.

We seem to be in a dark age when it comes to receiving revelation and new understanding for the manifestation of glory. Who will go before and open up our capacity to receive?

It is not that God has less to give. He can only give in relation of our capacity to receive. It is just like what occurred with the widow of Zarephath, to whom Elijah gave instructions to borrow containers. She was told to shut the door and pour her oil into the vessels. When the containers were full, "the oil was stayed."

Oil in biblical usage is symbolic of the Holy Spirit. The Holy Spirit is being poured out through intercession in private. The hidden ministry of intercession is being manifested in visible outpourings. Because the hidden work of "pouring out the oil into vessels" is not seen or is "behind the door," we try to explain all spiritual phenomena from the point of the manifestation.

Spiritual outpourings from past revivals have been analyzed on the basis of visible experiential manifestation. Books are written in corroboration with observable human experience, intellect, and rationale. Every new revival gives critics more material to write on.

Of recent years there have been some strange spiritual manifestations to accompany them. One such revival, the Toronto Blessing of 1994, created a fair bit of stir in the Christian community. A new drug—some called it "spiritual ecstasy"—seemed to be handed out to the people being "slain in the spirit." While under the power, people would have sensations of being bathed in love, rapturous joy, or heavenly tranquility.

Along with these experiences came the bizarre. Some people would bark while others roared. Some people would cry out while others would shake their arms as though they felt fire. A man would run with arms outstretched as though he was flying through the air like an eagle. Other manifestations saw people jerking, shaking, or bending over as though in the pangs of birth.

Were these fleshly indulgences or hypnotic manifestations of the Devil? Paul talked about persons making a "fair show in the flesh." However, this was not the drama that visiting evangelists or even local pastors were really in control of. Many manifestations occurred of their own volition through attending naive congregants and God-seeking people.

The Spirit of God should not contradict the Word of God. Either we are missing it entirely, or we may need to reorder ourselves and adjust our minds to the supernatural. Clearly some elements are counterfeits, but in some instances what we perceive as counterfeits may not be that at all. They may be real confrontations of the Holy Spirit in communication through the human spirit in ruling and dealing with the ranks of evil.

The Bible makes it clear that a high level of organization is at work against us. This underworld of malevolent activity requires methodic strategizing at the highest levels of operations. Upper boardroom meeting between Satan and his ruling fallen angels are certainly part of the "principalities and powers" strategy to network their specialties. (See Ephesians 6:12.)

How does man play into this? Worship is communicated through language and voice. Even music must have a voice. The gifts of the Holy Spirit, particularly through manifestations, are released through voice and action. Our bodies are His temples and vehicles for transmission.

One particular gift is the utterance gift of tongues for warfare in dealing with the Devil. These are gifts from the Holy Spirit for the benefit of the church in building the kingdom of God.

The kingdom of Satan has similar gifts. He also communicates through supernatural language and hypnotic trance. The blood of Christ is our protection, and the gift of discerning of spirits makes them very evident.

Paul said we are "an evident token of perdition" (Philippians 1:28) to them. In other words, they know they are on the path to spiritual ruin. We are not frightened, timid or taken in by guile or deception. We have not the spirit of fear but of power, love, and a sound mind.

We also know people by their fruit and can sometimes even know things about the condition of a person's spiritual state through an inward witness. The Devil has purported some of his tactics through lying wonders and lofty speculations with new-age philosophies that appeal to the flesh realm.

One example is the daily newspaper. How many persons make it a regular part of their morning routine to check their daily horoscopes? These astrological reports are part of Satan's lying wonders waiting to deceive the gullible because they carry a certain mystical element of truth. They hold no power unless people empower them in credence and belief. Prophecy must be affirmed by an inward witness. Otherwise it is of no consequence.

People are yearning for a glimpse into their future. Jeremiah 29:11 gives us a glimpse of the Father's will for us. It is God's desire to give us a hope and a future, but only through the leading of the Holy Spirit and His Word.

We are not to be ignorant of the Devil's devices. The problem with the Devil is that he has no creativity in him. He desires to be God, but he can only mimic or copy God. That is where the deception lies.

But we are of God. We have an "unction from Him and know all things." The Holy Spirit wants to give us an understanding and assurance that we are of the truth.

How are we to distinguish between the counterfeit and the real? This knowledge does not come through our senses or rational observation. This is the realm of deception. An underdeveloped spirit man will make us soul creatures that are not able to discern spiritual activity. The mind that is not renewed is against God.

Discernment is an operation of faith that comes from our spirits. As our minds are renewed to the Word of God, it becomes like a sword that is more able to discern and "rightly dividing between soul and spirit… and is a discerner of the thoughts and intents of the heart" (Hebrews 4:12). Paul says we are to be renewed in the spirit of our minds. That is the key.

CHAPTER 2
SPEAKING IN TONGUES? NEVER!

Many years ago in a small Mennonite community church, a member, during the service, began to publicly speak in tongues. The church was held in the grip of terror for a minute. That poor soul who had so dared to imperil himself in a Mennonite church had no idea what was in store for him. There was no attempt made at interpretation. The people were aghast by the audacity and impropriety of the whole outburst.

Well, it had gotten the people all riled up during the week, so the next week there was an announcement from the pulpit. "There would be no more speaking in tongues in that church."

This was an extreme phobic reaction. From this to others incidents where there just seems to be random chaos in some charismatic meetings, we need further understanding as to what tongues are all about.

In beginning an explanation on tongues, we need to have some biblical understanding as to the person and work of the Holy Spirit.

The Work and Person of the Holy Spirit

The Holy Spirit in many denominations is referred to as *it*, merely an ethereal presence of sort. Because He (the Holy Spirit) does not speak of Himself but on behalf of another (Christ), we do not recognize that He has a personality. In saying this, we are not separating the oneness of the Godhead. Jesus did the express will of the Father. The Holy Spirit is "Christ in us, the hope of glory."

We may see some characteristics of the Holy Spirit as in natural relationships. When someone loves greatly, there is deep hurt and grief attached to rejection. This is one characteristic of the person of the Holy Spirit and one secret to carrying His presence. He is the Comforter (*paraclete*[5] in Greek), meaning one who walks alongside us to help us in our daily walk. He has come to be with us forever, to give us a hope and a future. He will rest upon us if we come to revere His holy presence.

It is not only the grieving but the quenching that stops Him from releasing His mighty acts. Various kinds of tongues are another dimension to the manifestation of His power and presence.

I have wondered both at how He speaks through our voice not only to deal with the Devil but to inspire and equip us to pray. The voice of the Lord is powerful, and the voice of the Lord is full of majesty. Psalm 29 describes that voice. Psalm 92:10 says we shall be strengthened "with the strength of a unicorn."

Fresh oil will equip us for battle. "The yoke shall br destroyed because of the anointing oil" (Isaiah 10:17). The anointing oil yokes us to Christ. Oil in nature breaks down, and oil may leak. We may need an oil change, a revival. Or we may need a fresh fill of oil to free us from old patterns that have left us rigid, ineffective, and

---

[5] 3875 Greek lexicon, *Strong's Concordance*.

unyielding. When we minister to others, we pour out oil. We will need seasons of refreshing and refilling.

The Holy Spirit is the resident presence of Christ. He yokes us to Christ. He is represented by the anointing oil. The blood of Christ restores us to our relationship with Him. The anointing oil seals us with His presence.

The Holy Spirit is displayed in the mighty acts of the apostles. It is the Holy Spirit that pursues and convicts us of sin. It is He that has ownership and seals us unto the day of redemption.

It is the Holy Spirit that empowers us in the same way to live this life free from addictions. He that raised Christ from the dead is able to make alive our mortal bodies. That is freeing our bodies from compulsive bondage.

The Holy Spirit is the tangible presence of Christ. We cannot present our bodies to God without Him. Jesus is standing on our behalf interceeding in high priestly advocacy forever. He is interceding through us in the power and person of the Holy Spirit through mighty tongues of fire and revelation.

When we come into His presence with our own agendas and expect Him to bless it, the Holy Spirit is quenched. He may still bless us, but He is not present in a tangible way.

Moses longed for the tangible presence of God because He had experienced Him in the desert with the burning bush. When we have experienced God in a tangible way, we will become addicted. Moses' face glowed with the tangibility of God's presence. How much more should we burn with His fire and glory, we who are purged from our old sins and bought with the precious blood of Christ.

I am convinced there is nothing greater than the tangible presence of God. He is wonderful, real, and full of beauty. I have also felt his burning inside on my face, neck, and ears.

Warmth and feelings of being bathed in love describe some people's encounters with the tangibility of His presence. His power through intercession is explosive. The voice of the Lord is powerful. (See Psalm 29.)

The servant Elisha saw God move through Elijah the prophet, and he was hooked. We can read about the dialogue between Elisha and Elijah in 2 Kings 2. Elijah tells Elisha to wait by the river, while he went on. Elisha essentially said, "Nothing doing, I am not leaving you, my lord." Another time Elijah says, "Stay at the brook while I go on." Elisha would have said, "No, I am sticking to you like glue."

We need to have that kind of tenacity when it comes to the anointing. People will drive for miles to get under the anointing of a man of God just to experience a touch from God. One touch from God can change a life forever.

In this account, we read that after a chariot of fire had swept away the old prophet, the mantle fell from his body. Elisha picked it up. He knew it was his tangible link to the anointing.

Each of us has a tangible link to the anointing. For Moses, it was his staff. God said, "Throw down your staff." It became a snake. He told him to "pick it up again," and it became a staff again. It became the visible and tangible link for the supernatural deliverance he was to bring to the children of Israel.

God asks us, "What is in your hand?" Sometimes we do not even recognize what God is anointing.

We need to ask as Elisha did, "Where is the God of the apostles?" Jesus demonstrated through mighty acts that He was the God and Savior of this world. Can we do less as His followers? We need to take His mantle (the Holy Spirit) and begin to speak His Word into the earth. He is here. We are His body, the church.

In our churches He is available but not accessible. We have not regarded His presence. "Holy and reverend is His Name" (Psalm11:9). We have lost our reverence to wait for Him.

People should be bringing the sick to church every Sunday. So many emotional problems and familial relationships could be solved with an entrance into His glory. The hardness of people's hearts, which is responsible for so much divorce and heartache, could be melted in a moment. Years of neglect and emotional pain could be resolved from one encounter with Christ in the presence of His Holy Spirit.

How can we bring the tangible presence of God into our church? We must have both a regard for His presence and an allowance for the gifts of utterance to bring breakthrough and manifestation.

CHAPTER 3

TWENTY-ONE (PLUS ONE) GIFTS OF THE SPIRIT FOR THE CHURCH

There are twenty-one gifts of the spirit for the leadership, function, and building of the church. We may see them in operation every day, but these are indeed supernatural gifts They require that particular anointing that effectually works in every member. Tradition teaches only nine gifts of the Spirit. (see 1 Corinthians 12:28.) A figurative spiritualizing of the power gifts, the gifts of utterance and manifestation will miss our Ascended Lords revelation through Paul to the Church. We need to apply a consistent literal grammatical hermeneutic to restore where we are at today.

The Holy Spirit

Ultimately the Holy Spirit is the earnest of our possession (the guarantee of our inheritance), the treasure we find in a field and sell all our possessions to buy. He is the treasure that dwells in earthen vessels (us) whereby "we cry Abba Father." It is by Him that we are adopted into the family as sons (or heirs) and baptized into one body, the head being Christ. It is essential to recognize that it is not so much the numerous gifts but the sole gift that we must seek.

Administration

The reason we don't see the fivefold leadership move very powerfully is because we don't honor them and esteem the gifts God has placed in His body. When we honor the gift, we essentially pull on the anointing that is in and upon them.

The five designated offices of administration are the visible leaders of the church—the apostles, prophets, evangelists, pastors, and teachers. These are listed in Ephesians 4:11. These essential anointed offices are the framework of the body. Without them there will be limitations and error.

False humility errs when it puts emphasis on the priesthood of all believers above the selection of God's own choosing. When we ordain carpenters and tradesmen, into offices they were never called to perform we grieve the Spirit of God. When we supplant anointing with prominence, whether it be professors, musicians or successful business persons, we miss the sanctity and purity of this foundational structure.

Operations

Another listing of gifts in Romans 12:6–8 could be labeled the *operation of the church*. These are outlined and utilized by seven characteristics. They include the following: proclaiming, serving, teaching, encouraging/exhorting, giving, leading, and showing mercy.

Similar qualities may accompany and involve characteristics of the fivefold administrative gifts, but they are separate from the fivefold ministry in their specific operations.

For example, one may teach but primarily be called to pastor. One may prophesy but not be used in ministry as a prophet. Others may show mercy or be involved in any of the operations of service yet be more specifically called to administration.

A prophetic gift may have two sides. It may comfort, restore, and affirm yet have a fierceness when it is exposing sin and error. As an example, consider David, who was the sweet psalmist of Israel. He sang about the mercies of God, yet he was a warrior against injustice and evil.

Manifestations

The third designation is manifestations. These nine gifts are more visible, enjoying more acclaim, yet it is the same Spirit at work. These are outlined in 1 Corinthians 12:7–10.

Classified into three groups, the gifts of manifestation are utterance gifts, power gifts, and gifts of revelation. The *utterance* gifts consist of *tongues, interpretation of tongues, and prophecy.* The *power* gifts include *healing, working of miracles, and the gift of faith.* The gifts of *revelation* consist of the *word of knowledge, a word of wisdom, and discerning of spirits.*

By faith we understand that the worlds were framed by the Word of God (see Hebrews 11:3). Words are essential in declaring, ruling, and setting boundaries that the Enemy cannot pass over. Words are essential in birthing and creating—first the spiritual and then the natural.

This is one reason the Enemy has sought to muffle the gifts of utterance. We stress love as the greatest gift, with all the schmoozing of sloppy agape. We have lost power to a nation that exalts tolerance above truth. We are not saved by love. We are saved by blood. Words (the utterance gifts) are essential to the power gifts and the gifts of revelation.

Miracles: Gifts of Healing

Evangelists will often move in the area of miracles as did Philip of Samaria. Evangelists draw attention and acclaim to the gospel. Evangelists enjoy the spectacular and garner and capitalize on sensation.

Conversely the pastor may never see a miracle in his ministry. His ministry may be no less supernatural, just that it is not as visible. The pastoral ministry is of equal significance. It has a different purpose that is no less important.

The nature of ministry is that it has with it a special grace to minister within its order, function, and operation. A pastor may see a lot of tangible healing in his church through the laying on of hands. It may not always be the lead pastor who has remarkable answers to prayer. It may be the assistant who enjoys more acclaim because he is involved in dealing with the people's problems. He is praying with his flock. The pastors need to love and nurture the sheep. The lead pastor may be more employed in writing sermons and influential in providing leadership and feeding the body. His position might be lonelier, but He has to be the visionary leader. That is why sometimes there are pastoral teams.

The pastor is the shepherd that guides, guards, feeds, and provides seed for his flock. He nurtures and provides a safe place and haven for his sheep. A pastor may see provision that others have to find on a different level.

Utterance Gifts

The utterance gifts of tongues and interpretation, prophecy, wisdom or a word of knowledge has been severely limited in the body of Christ. The church has fearfully quenched the use and exploration of this blessing.

Growth and increase is a process that requires patience and time. Nobody arrives perfect in Christ. We are to come to a measure of greater stature and fullness in Christ. We yearn for such a state, but most persons must go through much trial and experimentation before they mature.

Even the gifts require experimentation, honing, and proving things out. If every feeble attempt at obeying God in this area is squashed, how can faith grow so that the gift becomes relevant and skilled in its operation?

For example, one church had a policy. When someone had a word of revelation in their church, whether wisdom, knowledge, or tongues and interpretation, the sound technicians would record it. Then the church board would have a meeting on it to see if it met their biblical criteria. If so, then they would publish it in the next week's bulletin.

What kind of person would think about the exploration of a gift under such scrutiny? That is excessive control. This allows no freedom to grow in the areas of the gifts of utterance. Abusive discipleship may say they are watching over your souls, but in reality they may be protecting their own reputations. Shepherding of this type is excessive, subversive, and smothering.

As another example, sometimes a person will utter two or three syllables and then say, "The Lord loves you. He wants to bless you," then he or she will cry some more with emotional drama. These deluded souls do this every Sunday and are then held in esteem for their great spirituality. We have not entered into the power of the Spirit in this area.

Most persons have not been taught their need to strengthen themselves in the gifts of utterance, the Holy Spirit, and the Word.

In the natural, men stay in the more comfortable world of images and objects. They find respect in their jobs, so they are passive leaders at home. They may stimulate their emotional lives with recreational activities and find some fulfillment in companionship around those areas.

Women need to feel needed, so they fill their emotional reservoirs by talking on the phone about feelings, speculations, romance, or relationships.

We supplant the real gift with feeble fixes, messages from emotionally driven, spiritless, and needy persons. Many times these persons have a culpability for acclamation or an unmet interpersonal need at home.

This might be why persons instated into leadership in the church should have their own families in order before they lead others in the church. It is interesting how people get their needs mixed up and think being fulfilled or used in some great way at church will make up for their ineptitude at facing their situations at home.

Tongues and Interpretation

Paul put some limitations on these gifts with some of these things in mind. Some of the pandemonium was flesh-driven rather than spiritually inspired.

When he said tongues and interpretation should be by two or three, he wasn't making a law out of it. It was more of a guide to avoid or limit confusion.

Some of the tongues and interpretations people begin with are many times just people experimenting. We need to wait till the real gift flows. That might take more than two or three tries.

We like to have legalistic formulas. Somehow they make us more secure. Paul even adds later, "But ye may all prophesy one by one."

That is certainly more than two or three, but not all at once in every service. Have some order. Paul especially encouraged everyone to excel in the gift of prophecy (see 1 Corinthians 14:3) so that all would be comforted. He urges us to covet earnestly (or excel in) the best gifts (see 1 Corinthians 12:31a). The motivation is found in the chapter that follows—the love chapter of 1 Corinthians 13. The gifts must minister out of a pure heart.

One other consideration in ministering to the body in the area of the gifts of utterance and revelation is this: "If there be no interpreter present, then let him keep silent." That may specifically be one who interprets tongues, but the same might apply to one being present who is able to interpret what the Holy Spirit is doing in a service. Paul also puts this gift into perspective when he says in 1 Corinthians 14:19, "Yet in the church I had rather speak five words with my understanding, that by my voice I might teach others also, than ten thousand words in an unknown tongue." This particular gift is also portrayed as a sign to the unbeliever that may be present.

CHAPTER 4

BORN TO BE BROKEN, BROKEN TO BRING HEALING

As a young lad raised in a Mennonite church and community, I had lived a fairly sheltered life. Our family was very musical, my father being a piano tuner as well as a talented musician. My mom played the piano accordion too.

We had this old pump organ at home, which I spent many an hour playing. One of the songs I played was "Nur Nimm denn Meine Hende," which was a song of consecration with a chorus, "Lord, take then my hands and use them for your glory."

Sometimes when I would play, I would sing what we called "singing crazy." This kind of singing was not in English but was just whatever came to me. I believe that somewhere during my childhood the Lord gave me the ability to sing in the Spirit. I have no recollection of there being a specific event or time of receiving the gift and overflow of tongues, just that there would be an anointing to play music.

The Holy Spirit drew me in again at the beginning of the Word of Faith Movement. A great desire and thirst for the Word characterized this movement. I would listen to anointed teachers for hours a day, while I worked on pianos in my piano shop. Those were also days of a lot of prayer in the spirit and tongues.

An experience that would change my life significantly occurred during this period in my early adult life. I had rarely said a word all through my life growing up in Rosenfeld, Manitoba. I cannot recall ever asking a question in my classroom at school. I was quiet, extremely shy, and introverted, and yet I was zealous for God.

It was early adulthood. I had called a prayer meeting. A couple of my siblings and mom were there along with some neighboring folk. As we were together in God's presence, I began to sob. I had never been seen to show emotion in front of my family, and I would have rather died than show that kind of weakness. This was an incredible breaking through of the Holy Spirit in my life. I cried so hard. I just kept wailing out of control. I could not stop for what seemed hours, but I am sure was not that long.

The Holy Spirit broke me there, and He did a deep inward work, replacing my "stony heart with a heart of flesh." My heart was changed, but it was by the Holy Spirit's intervention.

The illustration of wine is in Acts 2, where people thought the disciples were drunk. They weren't drunk but became filled with new wine. Wine does to the flesh what the Holy Ghost does to the spirit.

When we get full of the Holy Ghost, it will affect our flesh and spill over from our spirits into every other parts of us. Ephesians 5:19 talks about "speaking to yourselves in psalms and hymns, making melody in your heart," which is something a drunk man would do. Out of the overflow of our hearts we begin to make melodies, sing, and dance. We become impervious to the stares of social impropriety and stigma.

Wine is another one of Satan's counterfeits. The Holy Spirit is the real deal. We need not settle for less.

In order to reuse old wineskins, they need to be rubbed in oil and saturated with water (representing the Word) so that they can stretch again. That is what Jesus meant when He said that old wineskins cannot contain what God wants to do.

We have to be expandable in our capacity to receive the Word. That is what tongues do in our lives. Part of the breaking of our vessel involves having to always do things out of our intellect and reasoning. Tongues helps us because we become aware of another dimension. Jesus came to heal all that were oppressed of the Devil. Tongues help us enter in to that anointing.

Eight Kinds of Tongues

During one Saturday night of prayer with other intercessors, we were moving in aggressive (militant) tongues. The word *natas* was prevalent in the utterance. One of the other intercessors later said, "That is Satan spelled in reverse." The Enemy may try to beguile us, but is no match for the Holy Spirit in us. Militant intercession is one dimension of tongues.

The diversity of operations spoken of in 1 Corinthians 12:6 includes the various or diverse kinds of tongues indicated in verse 10. The utilization of each of these is diverse and unique. It's design is for a particular operation.

Some types may flow more consistently in the life of the believer, depending on the implementation of the Holy Spirit. Our part lies in expectation as well as instrumentation, strategy, maturity, and tuning in to the use of the gift.

Spiritual warfare may include the understanding but has a dimension where people must trust their inward voice or unction. This is particularly essential when we are moving into militant tongues. They are specific in function and utterance and sometimes will include names and commands. This may not always be revealed to our understanding.

The eight categories I have given for tongues include the following:

Tongue for Revelation

This is an utterance by which we pray under the influence and illumination of the Holy Spirit. I believe there is a relationship between tongues and the other utterance gifts. There is a significant order when Paul says in 1 Corinthians 12, "I will pray with the spirit, and I will pray with the understanding... I will sing with the spirit, I will sing with the understanding." A word of wisdom, word of knowledge, or prophecy may be regarded as the tongues of men, where the word is given with supernatural insight and clarity. This ties in with being able to interpret one's own prayers where Paul says in 1 Corinthians 14:13, "Let him that speaks in an unknown tongue pray that he may interpret."

Tongues of Men

This may be where some missionaries have preached in foreign countries in languages they have not learned and have not understood what they were saying. An instance might be where the nationals hear someone speaking in their dialect where the missionary has no knowledge whatsoever of whom they are addressing. This might parallel the experience in Acts where every foreigner heard them speak in their own national language.

Tongues of Angels

Paul said, "Though I speak with the tongues of men and of angels" (1 Corinthians 13). This tongue was for the purpose of employing angels. Hebrews 1:14 says, "Are they not all ministering spirits sent forth to minister for them who are heirs of salvation?" Hebrews 1:7 calls the angels "flaming messengers of fire." Psalm 103:20 says, "Bless the Lord ye his angels, that exell in strength, that do his commandments, hearkening unto the voice of his word."

The Father commissions the angels as the Holy Spirit prays for the perfect will of God through us. The presence of angels is part of the labor force negotiating God's workmanship in us. We may work out our salvation with fear and trembling, but we are not on our own. We are to fear and tremble at the Word of God, but we have an awesome task force in heaven that the intercession of the Spirit is making available for and through us. The plan that He has for us involves favor with God and man. Jesus said we are never on our own. He beheld Satan as lightning fall from heaven, while the seventy went out and ministered.

Praying in these kinds of tongues takes the limits off human knowledge, understanding, and expression. Angels are part of God's glory in heaven and brings His will and presence into the earth. We are His workmanship. When we work God works, He clothes himself with us. We are created for His glory. The presence of angels is not just a mystical emotion. They have strength and purpose, and they are on assignment.

One morning the Lord said to me in my spirit, "How many angels will I dispatch for you today?" In the workforce the foreman will say, "How many helpers will you need to do your job?" When we speak in our heavenly language, we (by the Holy Spirit) may be employing angels.

Tongues at the Baptism of the Holy Spirit (Acts 2:1–4)

Some have contested that tongues must accompany the baptism of the Holy Spirit. This first outpouring included tongues as many subsequent outpourings did in this instance. The Holy Spirit produces the utterance. This initial manifestation also requires the strength of our surrendered minds and voices. Psalm 51:15 says, "Open your mouth and I will fill it with praise." One experiment done by scientists at the University of Pennsylvania measures neuronal activity in the frontal lobes, the thinking wilful part of the brains. The brain imaging for this region was relatively quiet. Proverbs 20:27 says, "The spirit of man is the candle of the Lord searching all the inward parts of the belly." It is out of our spirits that we speak. Our minds are at rest (Isaiah 28:11, 12).

Tongues as a Sign to the Unbeliever (1 Corinthians 14:22)

This manifestation was subsequent to the initial upper-room baptism of fire where "tongues of fire sat on their heads." This instance of every man hearing them speak in their own language occurred outside as *a manifestation for street evangelism*. The evangelist garners more attention through miracles, signs, and wonders because he is getting the attention of the ungodly. This manifestation gathered attention and caused a perplexity in the crowds that had already gathered there. The noise of the wind (roar) of the Holy Spirit on people's hearts may have already drawn the people together.

The Tongue of Edification (Jude 20)

This tongue is instrumental in building up the believer in areas of faith. This type of praying is a catalyst in linking the natural to the supernatural. An anointing becomes resident and is released from our inner man as the need arises. Paul accessed this type of tongue when he said, "I pray in tongues more than you all."

Tongues for Interpretation (1 Corinthians 12:7–10)

Isaiah 28:11 refers to this manifestation of the spirit when he says, "With stammering lips and another tongue will He speak to this people." This manifestation is the corporate gift where prophetic insight, weight, or illumination of scripture may be released through interpretation. This is what a lot of people have in mind when they hear about speaking in tongues. This is a gift of revelation for the purpose of our understanding.

Militant Tongues

These tongues are attacking, confrontational, and aggressive in nature. This is a tongue the Devil (a fallen angel) understands. As we speak under the unction of the Holy Spirit in militant tongues, we are confronting the powers of darkness and taking authority over the kingdom of Satan. The Enemy is rebuked, and his strategies are despoiled. The Spirit of God raises up a standard of defense against him over which he must capitulate.

Power and Void Teaching

Paul warns Timothy of the power of God being made void through our traditions.

Dispensationalism teaches that healings and miracles have been relegated to a past apostolic age for the forming and establishing of the gospel. That age has purportedly passed since signs and wonders were necessary only for the writing and establishing of scripture. As we now have a completed copy of scripture, this enlightened age no longer needs signs and wonders to draw the attention of believers or unbelievers to the supernatural working of Christ.

Furthermore, the Word of God (including the book of Acts) is complete. We look for a future kingdom of restoration rather than a present reality of transformation. Power is an inward experience of regeneration. Power beyond that is excessive and doctrinally suspect.

Missionaries have gone to foreign lands and taught people that diseases came from germs, not by evil spirits as the nationals superstitiously thought. They preached assurance of spiritual salvation and good works but removed Him from much of any tangible intervention in the daily lives of the people.

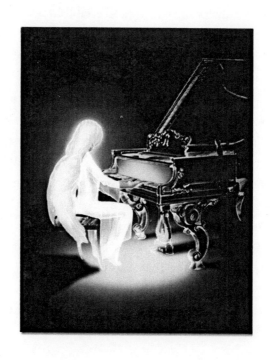

CHAPTER 5
MANIFESTATION IN RELATION TO HUNGER FOR GOD

Angels Tinkling the Piano Keys

A couple of times when I was asleep, I remember hearing piano keys in the top register tinkling at the other end of the house in my piano (prayer) shop. They woke me up for prayer.

I believe God (and His holy angels) were waking me. I think the Father longs for fellowship with us and waits for us in that certain place just as Jesus had communion with His Father on the Mount of Olives.

Desire and longing for God are what takes us farther than others. When we are desperate for God, then He becomes real to us.

Jesus' prayer in John 17 reveals some of the desperation and the longing of His heart. He longs to be with His Father and to share that communion with us. Even as we are in Christ and He is in the Father, we will have fellowship together. Through the indwelling Holy Spirit, they will come and make their abode with us.

We must hear the desperation for that relationship. It is like a man who is longing for his lover. His heart is reaching out to be near that other person just to hear her voice. Perhaps just one phone call.

Jesus wants to reveal to us His Father's will. He wants to talk to us every day. He longs for us when we haven't called.

The element of prayer in spiritual warfare is a subsequent part of that love relationship. It has been a precedent somewhere, with every major outpouring of the Holy Spirit. There is something about people who are hungry for God, who are desperate for His presence. The manifestation of God comes in relation to our hunger as well as our ability to contend against the forces of darkness.

This is not something that we do in our own strength. The apostle Paul says specifically that our fight is not in the flesh but has a spiritual origin. Ephesians 6:12 says, "For we wrestle not against flesh and blood, but against principalities, against powers, against the rulers of the darkness of this world, against spiritual wickedness in high places."

The stewardship of every believer is to cleanse their vessels and offer them up in sanctification to God. Then as we come to the house of God and begin to offer up our sacrifices of praise, the spirit of glory can come down in greater power and manifestation.

Jesus wants His temple to be a house of prayer. Haggai 2:7 says, "The glory of this latter house shall be greater than of the former." God desires to manifest His glory more than we are ready to receive it.

There are some conditions that must be in place before this is to happen.

Glory and Gifting

The place of prayer is a habitation of the Spirit. He indwells us as we separate ourselves unto Him. As we repair the breaches of the temple walls, representing where the Enemy has had access in the past, we are then able to contain more glory.

How much glory we carry is significant to how far back we are able to push the Enemy. We have the Spirit in a measure.

Paul said that the gift of grace was given unto him according to the measure that he needed to minister as overseer over all the churches. Collectively as the body of Christ, we are to carry His Spirit, the Spirit without measure. Paul longed to impart some spiritual gift to the church. He longed to see them operating in the full measure of Christ. Paul had to have more grace in order to give more.

We need the gifts of administrations (Ephesians 4:11) for impartation. We recognize Christ has set a fivefold ministry into the church for the completion of the body. We also recognize that God moves and speaks through lines of authority.

Engagement with the Enemy

Authority is not enough. It must be implemented. Jesus has given us access to the Father by His blood. Although we have access, we do not affect spiritual power without some effort on our part. Audience with the Father is not in itself authority. We must fulfill our end of the covenant by enforcing that rule on the earth.

"Having boldness in the day of redemption, we have access through the blood of the everlasting covenant." We must affect that authority through a knowledge of our covenant rights as God's children. We must begin to understand the magnitude of the evil network assigned and assailed against the church.

All of life this side of heaven is warfare. The Enemy still has territorial claims that we must call into question. We must inform the Devil that his stage is a mere despot, that he is defeated. He must leave. His authority must be challenged with the Word of God and the blood of Christ. This enforcement is where militant intercession begins to engage specific entities in the spirit realm.

Evil princes and governments still control cities and countries. We must gain and enforce jurisdiction. Even though Jesus has given us the power, it is not automatically ours. This is where engagement is necessary. The sword of the Lord is the Word of God. We stretch out the sword of the Lord against the Enemy through prayer and declaration.

The battle is won on the basis of the blood of the everlasting covenant, but we are not exempt from the battle. We have all the tools for the battle. We must begin to utilize what is at our disposal. We have been in the woodsheds, rehearsing with wooden mallets. God has made the weapons of war available to us. We have not grasped what they are or how to use them.

The everlasting covenant is enacted through belief and confession. The Word of God is that covenant written on men's hearts as well as on paper. When it is spoken, it becomes life-giving. The same can be said of words. Once they are spoken, they are emboldened or filled with power. As God speaks through His children, His Word gives us the power to become the sons of God.

By His Word He breaks bands asunder. God is waiting patiently for the manifestation of the sons of God. As we speak His Word, we begin to manifest His Word just like Jesus did. Jesus was the firstborn of many brethren. We are to take His Word and His mantle and do His work with the sword of the Spirit, even greater works than those recorded in the Bible. How is this to be?

We know that no word of prophecy is of any private interpretation, but holy men of God spoke as they were moved by the Holy Ghost. So holy men are still speaking from the canon of scripture. They are speaking a word in season—a word of prophecy that is a present word, a word that brings into manifestation the glory and power of God. When we engage the Enemy, we speak the Word just like Jesus did in the wilderness of testing.

We do not always know how to adequately Engage the enemy, as this is a spiritual fight. That is why we need tongues. As we pray to the realm of the Spirit, the Holy Spirit begins to assist us in our prayer. He may give us special insight into how to pray, but He also begins to engage the Enemy for us. He has the knowledge and strategy we need to pull down the strongholds.

Sometimes all it takes is coming together in communion with our bodies, our consecration, and our prayer language. As God begins to fill us with the Holy Spirit for engagement with the Enemy, we speak forth an utterance that dispels and demolishes Satan's kingdom. While this may involve some mental engagement, it is primarily spiritual.

CHAPTER 6
OTHER MANIFESTATIONS IN SPIRITUAL INTERCESSION

I remember when the Holy Spirit was first poured out in a greater measure in an intercessory prayer group at our church years ago. The leader laid hands on a fellow who began to bellow like a moose. Something opened up and broke through in the spirit realm as though there were a supernatural outpouring. People started laughing uproariously in totally drunken behavior. It seemed like we graduated from one level of intercession into another.

None of us had ever experienced any of these things before. From the laughter we went to groaning, to travailing, and then to weeping. Some began speaking in really different kinds of tongues.

One fellow, a construction worker, had these tongues like a machine gun going off. I thought, *That is not speaking anything. He just sounds like a machine gun.* I realized we had entered into spiritual intercession and engagement with the Enemy. We had entered into a new level of warfare. We had victory, and the Enemy was on the run.

That incredible release of spiritual power touched lives with an impact that lasted a lifetime. A great spiritual work followed in subsequent years, and it still remains today.

I have learned to recognize various utterances that have come through my spirit as an operation of a spiritual gift from God. One of the manifestations that comes only by the Spirit is groaning and travailing. Other manifestations, such as roaring and militant tongues, are parts of the voice and utterance that accompanies spiritual warfare. I feel there is scriptural precedence here.

Groaning in the Spirit

Romans 8:19–23 indicates that all creation is groaning and travailing in pain together, awaiting the glorious liberty of the children of God.

I equate groaning as though there is a huge weight that we are straining against. It is a spiritual work somewhat akin to the natural. It may begin with an initial effort that seems futile, but as we persevere together, straining against it with spiritual groanings, the Holy Spirit accomplishes the task. It may feel like too huge a task for us, but we must continue to strain as though we are pushing something forward in the spirit. Some of these things seem to take longer to move than we would like.

We may not always get a breakthrough on our time line, but that is not for us to decide. This is where we need people not to grow impatient and take over with their great minds but persevere until the spiritual work is accomplished. There will be a perceptible lightness and release when it is accomplished.

It may not always be that we experience a breakthrough. We may have to continue at another time. We need to realize that we are not in control, but the Holy Spirit knows what is necessary to accomplish the task. We have this treasure in earthen vessels. We must recognize our limitations.

Scripture refers to both a natural and a spiritual labor or birthing process in the Lord. Paul was zealous and had a mandate from God. He wrote to Timothy, "For therefore we both labour and suffer reproach… (1Timothy4:10). Paul said again in Galatians 4:19, "My dear children, for whom I travail in birth again until Christ be formed in you." There is a distinction between natural and spiritual effort, but the spiritual work will not distort the natural. We have jobs, families, and children. They play significant roles in our calling and identity.

Travailing in the Spirit

Travailing in birth often goes along with the groaning as though we are giving birth to something. It seems to proceed from the center of our beings or our bellies. Proverbs 20:27 says, "The spirit of man is the candle of the Lord searching all the inward parts of the belly."

The belly is where this intercession is birthed. This is the process of laboring/toiling. People may appear in pain and bent over as if in the pangs of childbirth.

Spiritual birth is a reality. Paul said to the Galatians, "I travail in birth again, till Christ be formed in you."

Roaring in the Spirit

A roar in the spirit is empowered by the Holy Spirit for conquest against His enemies. Isaiah 42:13 says, "The Lord shall go forth as a mighty man, he shall stir up jealousy like a man of war; he shall cry, yea, roar; he shall prevail against his enemies." The roar places a trembling over the ranks of the Enemy.

When God speaks in a roar, this is also a militant term used for placement, authority, and government. Hosea 11:10 says, "They shall walk after the Lord: he shall roar like a lion; when he shall roar, then the children shall tremble from the west. They shall tremble as a bird out of Egypt, and as a dove out of the land of Assyria, and I will place them in their houses, saith the Lord."

Some *roaring* can be followed up with prophecy as in Amos 3:7, 8, which says, "Surely the Lord God will do nothing, but he revealeth his secret unto his servants the prophets. The Lion hath roared, who will not fear? The Lord God hath spoken, who can but prophesy?"

Prophesy is one dimension of God uttering His voice. When the Lord roars against His enemies in spiritual intercession, the Enemy trembles in the face of God's children. God anoints us in militant intercession with a roar for conquest.

The voice of the Lord in Psalm 29 thunders. It is powerful and full of majesty. It breaks the cedars, divides the fire, and shakes the wilderness. Surely a Spirit-empowered utterance (e.g., roar) will incite sheer terror into the camp of the Enemy.

An example of a New Testament roar occurred on the day of Pentecost (Acts 2:2). It says, "And suddenly there came from heaven a noise like a violent rushing wind, and it filled the whole house where they were sitting."

The Greek word for rushing is *phero*. It also means to carry or to bring forth. A noise could also be a roar.

There was a violent activity from heaven. It upset the regional powers that were accustomed to ruling there. The murderous atmosphere of the city, where just days ago they had crucified Jesus, turned to one of softening in their hearts and seeking God. The noise (roar), like a rushing wind, summoned people from all over the city. It blew conviction into the hearts of the people. Peter could preach, and three thousand souls would come to know the Lord.

Militant Tongues

Spiritual tongues are as real as any word of prophecy in a known language. They are a spiritual language designed for a spiritual purpose. The Devil has a language. We can speak to him in a militant tongue, which is one way we defeat his strategies. Christians can strategize together against the Devil. He is in utter chaos.

I was in a psychiatric ward in Calgary one day on visitation. There was a nice fellow there. The lady I had come to see said he spoke German. I talked to him and realized he was not speaking German but was speaking in tongues. So I spoke back to him in tongues. It was like we were having a conversation neither of us understood. It released great joy in that place. He had a guitar, and we sang some songs after.

Spiritual Barking

This is an odd manifestation, but there is a biblical reference in Isaiah 56. In this passage the Bible talks about God's house being a house of prayer. Here His watchmen (intercessors that keep a prayer vigil) are asleep. They are like "dumb dogs that cannot bark" (Isaiah 56:10).

This could be a warfare term dealing with the rooting out of unruly and unlawful spirits in God's house. We must recognize that dealing with the Devil is dirty business. His demons are unclean, rude, and crude. We as New Testament priests must disband, dispel, and dismantle the plans of our barbarous adversary.

An example of Satan's tactics might be seen in how he beguiles those seeking spirituality, where he shows up as a personal friend, a spirit guide from the past, or a grandfather. These sinister guides are the new-age replacement for the Holy Spirit. They have been around. This is why they are called familiar spirits. Nevertheless, they are intruders. A watchdog will drive them away.

Where manifestations like barking have been present, alongside these strange occurrences there have been great outpourings of the Holy Spirit. This only makes sense as it relates to spiritual warfare between that of an enemy that holds regions captive and our ability to loosen the hold the Enemy has on it.

It has never been God holding back from us. We have an open heaven. There is always an adversarial strategist (1 Peter 5:8) at work to distract us from receiving from God. Second Corinthians 4:4 says, "Of whom the God of this world hath blinded the minds of them which believe not, lest the light of the glorious gospel of Christ who is the image of God should shine unto them."

It is up to us to employ the Holy Spirit in power, master strategy and engagement against the vast network and determination of the Enemy. We give authority to the open heaven that is over our lives, to increase in territorial reign over our city. If we will not pray, He cannot move. The manifest presence will be ours, but we will never see it on a corporate level.

One of the major tactics of the Enemy is perpetrated through dividing and conquering God's people. Conservative people have difficulty assimilating manifestations with logic and believable faith. Yet that is where the power lies. It is in perceiving God is at work and believing that God is taking us out of the natural and into the supernatural.

It is essential to reintroduce the book of Acts into our subjective experience. God has not found it necessary to write any more scripture, but the reality is that He is writing through us a new page of history every day. No previous generation will write it for us. It will require the effort of our seeking God and what He is telling us to do. This is what is recorded in the book of remembrance in Malachi 3:16.

Our adversary works against us to bring this work of God to destruction. One of the tactics is to blind people from hearing and seeing the salvation of God. We need to be watchmen on the alert, to be sober and vigilant against an adversary that seeks to inspire fear and accusation (as a roaring lion) against us.

Ephesians 6:12 says that we wrestle against principalities, powers, and rulers of the darkness of this world. If they (this hierarchy of evil) want to operate in their world, they can, but in our world we must blind them with the blood of Jesus Christ. In my prayer time I always blind the Enemy with the blood of Jesus Christ. Then I pray in the Spirit. He is confused, and I am edified (Jude 20).

Counterfeit Spiritual Experiences

We are warned of counterfeit spiritual experiences. I think mature Christians can usually tell more easily when a demon is in operation from the emotional elements that are otherwise not as easily recognizable. This is where we are learning to recognize God's voice and beginning to distinguish that from ours.

With practice, we can develop discernment. Hebrews 5:14 says, "Who by reason of use, have their senses exercised to discern both good and evil." Through this we are developing our sensory organs and recognizing physical signs just as an airline pilot is trained to recognize his or her body signals when he or she is low on oxygen.

It is not with our own cognition, knowledge, or degrees that we are enabled to hear God's voice and engage in warfare. It is those who have exercised their spirit man and have learned to listen for God's voice. These may receive revelation in their inward man. These have presented their "threshing instrument with many sharp teeth" ready to "tear the enemy apart and make chaff of mountains" (Isaiah 41:15 NLT).

CHAPTER 7

IN THE MUD ROOM

On the farms we used to have a room for cleaning ourselves up from the barn before we entered the house. Spiritual warfare needs a room like that. Intercession and the deliverance ministry can be a dirty business. It does not have to be in front of TV cameras with critics and fancy suits.

At one church meeting I was in during some personal altar ministry, a lady intercessor in our church was interceding for someone with spiritual blindness. She was receiving an intercessory burden for an individual being ministered to at the front during special prayer. Her discernment was correct and spiritual insight right on, but her intercession was not understood.

The spirit of the prophet is subject to the prophets. Sometimes we just have to give it up. Some things are not worth the fight when you consider the effect something will have on your home or family. This lady was reproached and ostracized by others in the church. Most people have little understanding of intercession or the realm of the spirit.

That was somewhat of a strange occurrence that few understood. Perhaps there should be a side room for this type of ministry (if it was recognized). The main meeting should focus on worship, preaching, or personal ministry through the gifts of the Spirit. Healings and manifestations will be much more prevalent and vital when they have been birthed in intercession.

Individual people will act differently when the power of God *hits* their unrenewed flesh. It may be that some have spiritual impulses to run *Jesus laps* around the auditorium. Some persons will laugh or cry in deep emotional release. Others in intercession may be in deep travail or convulsing as if they are giving birth. Uproarious laughter and drunken behavior may overtake some as they encounter the Holy Spirit in their bodies.

The voice of the Lord breaks the cedar (Psalm 29). The voice of the Lord roars upon the waters. When the Lord roars, it is a sound heard in the spirit realm. His voice is heard and has conquest over the kingdoms of darkness.

So often we think it is our eloquence that can move the spirit realm. There is an eloquence empowered by God that reaches into the realm of the spirit, but not all speaking is of any particular significance. It may be a word of prophecy, but not all words carry any weight or are directed against the Enemy.

An interesting comparison is made in Mark 11:25 about the power of words in our regular speaking with words that have power and unction in our spiritual lives. All words are not effective in both worlds. This verse says, "If you say unto this mountain, be thou removed and cast into the sea, and doubt not in your heart, but believe the thing (*which you say* in your regular speech) will come to pass, you shall have (*whatsoever you say* when it really counts)".

It is interesting to note how many ministers of God don't have strong spirits. This can only come through praying in tongues and spending time in prayer, rehearsing God's Word. Jude 20 holds the key, "But you beloved, building up yourselves on your most holy faith, praying in the spirit."

Some speaking or preaching is to build up the strength and arsenal of the believer. We must contend for the Word and be built up in the inner man to withstand fiery darts. We must also have a well flowing out of us and a river (of supernatural anointing) whenever we need to be able to release a volley of Word against a particular stronghold of the Devil.

In North America we can live fairly well, choosing not to enter into warfare. We may choose to medicate ourselves with material possessions, the arts, or the media. We may feel autonomous in the way we work and provide for ourselves. God sometimes will let us live in our deluded state for a while. The Enemy does not hinder us, as we represent little effect or threat against him.

The man (or woman) of God (2 Timothy3:17) and thoroughly furnished for every good work must be a person with a heart for warfare. The Enemy does not rest for long. We may have times of rest and refreshing, but we never leave our spiritual work for a second. Jesus spent the whole night in prayer after some of His greatest successes. Consider the time when He fed the five thousand.

Manifestations at the Toronto Blessing

James Beverly in his investigative report of the Toronto Blessing talks about bizarre manifestations.[6]

> For example, many people in worship engage in high speed shaking of their hands, arms and head. Others make various chopping and swinging motions. Such actions can take place at various times in the evening meetings. People so engaged may be seated, standing or lying on the ground.

---

[6] Beverly, James A., *Holy Laughter and The Toronto Blessing*, Zondervan Publishing House, Grand Rapids, MI, 1995.

Still others have roared like lions or barked like dogs. I have personaly heard both in various meetings. I also heard one man making noises like a cow. Others have reported people oinking like pigs and crowing like roosters. These animal noises have created the most disgust among some critics.

Beverly says the dog barking is linked to a famous historical Kentucky revival, while the roaring is said to be a prophetic action to signal a powerful word from Jesus, the lion of the tribe of Judah.

I have my reservations about creating natural explanations for everything. Some persons are undoubtedly caught up in all the hype and elation. In a party atmosphere people become less inhibited and do funny things. This may account for some of the barnyard sounds. It is essential to recognize that all creation does have a voice. It groans together as it expectantly awaits its redemption. Even Jesus said that if we did not praise Him, the rocks would cry out. God is not religious in the slightest.

Some of the manifestations in the Toronto Blessing were quite crude, such as when one barker lifted his leg and pretended to urinate. Outraged leaders objected and reprimanded the disgusting behavior. "We are, after all, talking about worship in the presence of God."[7]

My feeling is that within the context there was some amount of bedlam. God is not nervous. We need to observe the larger picture. Jesus died a cruel, bloody death to redeem us from a dirty, diabolical entity. Demons are not pretty. To symbolically urinate on them may have the appearance of carnality, but the conquest is real. We need to be less tolerant of his nasty impositions in our lives and to have open disgust for the Devil! The reality is, though, that it is the blood of Christ that gives us authority over him.

---

[7] Ibid., pg.73.

Bizarre Spiritual Manifestations

Totally rational human beings have difficulty with these animal noises... and for good reason. Man was created in the image and likeness of God to exercise authority over the animal kingdom. To think that the Holy Spirit would degrade us to cause us to act like animals is inconceivable. It is also of interest that most references to dogs in the Bible paint them in an unclean, demeaning manner.

Casting out animal spirits is done in countries like Africa. People have worshipped animals or eaten their organs to partake of their spirit and fierceness. Some people will slither like snakes. I would have reservations if I saw a manifestation of this sort. One must not look at the manifestation but rather look inward to Jesus. If He is at the altar of our being where we worship; if He is the living resurrected Christ occupying our Holy of Holies, what is He doing, and what is He telling us to do?

There is no logical solution in attempting to rationalize animal noises. However, I believe that in the context of spiritual warfare, they play an authentic symbolic role.

If we are seeking the kingdom of God, we are in a relationship with God. We wear the robes of righteousness in Christ, and we are seated and reigning with Him from heavenly places. We must remember that in this lifetime we are dealing with very unclean spirits. Demons are a part of living and occupying the fallen state of the earth. Animal utterances are only part of God demonstrating that power and conquest over the demonic world.

Even speaking in erratic tongues has some persons disturbed. "It could not be a language," they say. "It is just repetitious nonsense." We know, however, that militant tongues are directed against the Devil. They are not a language for us to translate.

This can only be understood in the context of spiritual warfare. God is not particularly religious. Sometimes the Pharisees of today need to be undone with some valiant display of unorthodox behavior.

Decently and in Order

A clearer distinction needs to be made between worship services, all the other regular church stuff, and spiritual intercession. All meetings are not the same. There needs to be clearer delineation between services of orderly worship and spiritual warfare.

When one is engaging the Devil, worship may be involved but may not be evident as we know it in our church settings. All spiritual activity cannot be mixed together into one bowl. Just like there are different rules for different games or sports, so there is a diversity of directives involved for different activities or functions.

The Bible speaks of at least ten different types of prayer. We are to pray with all manner of prayer. The set of rules that govern (for example) the prayer of faith versus the prayer of consecration are opposite. The one is definite about receiving (Mark 11:24), while the other prays "if it be thy will." The two cannot be mixed together. Faith can only work where the will of God is known.

Using a similar thought, the emphasis of worship as we know it is not specifically warfare. Although worship certainly is warfare, we are not targeting ruling enemies, but we are extolling God.

Within that context, the Spirit of God may lift up a standard the Enemy cannot cross over (when the Enemy comes in like a flood). The purpose of worship (as we know it) is not to specifically root out enemy strongholds.

Although much of the content of a Sunday service is spiritual, not all activity is designed to achieve the same results. So warfare is not specifically worship, although all are under the same heading (just as sports are).

Holy Laughter

Powerful experiences of laughter swept whole crowds at the Toronto Airport Vineyard Church. This holy laughter would occur even during the preaching time. Sometimes preaching was taken over by this phenomenon. I think it has something to say about God. He has listened to enough dry sermons.

People would become spiritually drunk, falling over chairs or in the aisles. Even at they were staying home or at work or while they were driving, people would become drunk in the Spirit. (They were still in control of their mental faculties.)

It seems that the wine of the Holy Spirit has not run out. God is pouring out His Spirit upon *all* flesh. That is why the fields are ripe for harvest. The world is imploring God for spiritual manifestation.

Satan is making the most of this time of receptivity to spirituality. His psychics, gurus and manifestors of spirit guides are purloining the marketplace.

God is working to bring forth the maturity of the church. He is longing for the manifestation of the sons of God.

An authenticated disciple of Christ is to carry the presence of Jesus. We ought to fill the marketplace like Peter, where sick people are laid out in the streets, that even the shadow (tangible anointing) of Peter might pass over them and they would be healed.

We would like to monitor signs and wonders while the world is crying out, "Show me a God that is real!"

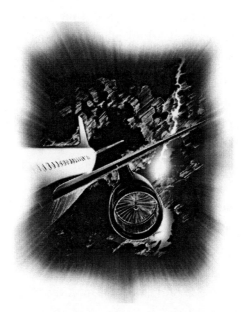

CHAPTER 8
PRAYER AND THE SOVEREIGNTY OF GOD

The Plane Roared Back up into the Sky

I remember one morning about 4:30 a.m. I was up to catch a flight to Calgary from Winnipeg for my graduation ceremony in Bible college. As was my custom, I would pray in the spirit for a while and walk the floor. As I was praying in tongues, I said, "It's canceled." I had a word of knowledge. This came to me three times. I said rather indignantly, "What's canceled?" I did not even trust my own voice or direction.

I went on the flight. All was fine till we got to Calgary. The plane got down within a hundred yards of the runway, and everything was a whiteout. We roared back up into the skies to Kamloops for refueling and then continued on to Vancouver. It took me three days to get back to Manitoba through Edmonton. Calgary was totally shut down with the worst snowstorm in ages.

I believe many calamities could be averted if one would take the time to pray in the spirit. Even some of the decisions we make, we get ourselves tied up in a lifetime of debt. If only Jesus said, "You had known the day of your visitation," then I would have covered you with wings as a mother her chicks.

We cannot ignore God's provision for our lives. Part of that is entering into the utterance gifts with revelation, including the word of wisdom and the word of knowledge.

Tongues: A Tangible Link for the Supernatural

God requires man to be a part of the process. That is one reason we speak in tongues. Tongues are a connection between the supernatural and the natural. There needs to be a point of contact. Words are that point of contact.

An example is in receiving salvation. If a man believes in his heart and confesses with his mouth, he shall be saved. Both word and action are involved. There must be a witness in the earth for heaven to be released. Words become the legal document that releases divine mysteries into the earth.

This is not to say that God does not hear silent prayers from our hearts, but prayers have more power when spoken out loud. It is as if there needs to be a witness or tangibility that brings authority into this world.

Words are given authority when they appear in the physical world. After the Spirit of God moved upon the face of the deep, God spoke, "Light be," and there was light. Even though there is a hidden work of the spirit, it is when the prophetic (*rhema* in Greek) word is spoken that the power inherent within the words are released.

The basis of some faith movements had this emphasis—that faith comes by hearing and hearing by the Word of God. Faith does not necessarily come by reading, although reading inspires hope. People are saved by the preaching of the gospel and the hearing of an anointed Word or message. Faith also comes when we rehearse God's Word in speaking it audibly to ourselves.

Romans 10:14, 17 indicates that the faith necessary for the ungodly to be saved comes by the preaching of the gospel. Some revelation comes through reading, but the speaking and physical hearing have a strong part in building faith for the Word to take root in one's heart.

This principle applies similarly to the process of memorization. It is very difficult to memorize something without speaking it out loud. Prayer and worship have a similar dimension. If all one ever does is pray in his or her heart, that person's expression will be limited as is his or her ability to receive from God.

Praying Mysteries

When I pray in tongues, Paul says in Romans 14:2 that I am praying mysteries. My soul, the perceivable part of me, is unedified. I am speaking mysteries into this earth by the spirit. Those mysteries are not just there to frustrate us. They are the revealed will of God in code. Some of these mysteries we can pray to interpret. Others come by way of revelation through our spirits. It is then that we are able to comprehend with all the saints what the riches of our inheritance in Christ are

It is not just God's desire to confuse us with mysteries. It is His desire to reveal them to us. This is a great tool in receiving revelation. It is when I speak in tongues that revelation knowledge comes to my mind. First Corinthians 2:9-10 says, "Eye hath not seen, nor ear heard, neither have entered into the heart of man, the things which God hath prepared for them that love Him, but God hath revealed them unto us by His Spirit..."

It is God's desire to unveil and reveal Himself to the children of men. Many Christians do not have the ability to attend theological seminaries, but they need not be disadvantaged. Through prayer and meditation in the Word as well as listening and studying anointed ministers of God, we receive revelation. That is not to say we should opt out of Bible School. This just implies personal responsibility and accessibility.

We cannot just read the Bible. We need the body with its administration in the fivefold ministry. These are there for the perfecting of the saints and for the work of the ministry. Without them, we will be incorrect in areas, lack sharpness, and come behind in the gifts of the Spirit.

Study must be accompanied with praying in the Holy Spirit. We pray with our spirits and then with our understanding. We sing with our spirits and then with our understanding. The order is significant. The first gives authority to the revelation, putting it into words (albeit unintelligible). Then we translate by praying into our native language.

Oral Roberts stated that this is how he received insight and planning in building the city of faith. He would walk the grounds, pray in tongues, and then ask God for the interpretation.

It would seem that this type of prayer with interpretation does not operate word for word. As I pray in tongues first, God gives me the inspiration and key to the next phase of operations. Sometimes it will be a specific word of knowledge or wisdom, but I think it is more about releasing a process of thought.

I feel that many dilemmas are solved after this order. We may walk the floor at night with something on our minds. As we pray in the Spirit, God gives a key scripture or thought to unfold the mysteries we are praying. It may even come as specific instructions to our understanding.

Paul says we ought to pray for the interpretation of our tongues for ourselves. This interpretation is more of an inspired prayer, perhaps even a prophetic prayer. Second Peter 1:19 tells us all scripture is prophecy. When we pray scripture, if it is "...rightly dividing the word of truth (1 Timothy 2:15), we are praying prophetically. The key is to pray the right scriptural admonition at the right time.

Peter said in 2 Peter 1:20, "No prophecy of the scripture is of any private interpretation, but holy men of God spake as they were moved by the Holy Ghost." There are still holy men speaking and moving by the Holy Ghost. They do not speak the Word for the purpose of writing scripture but for the purpose of presenting what is already revealed.

It is with the same authority they speak, than when scripture was written. Scripture is not selective when it comes to the inherent qualifying of men for holy apostles. They were the apostles of the Lamb, specifically chosen for a purpose. They were inspired by the same Holy Spirit that gives spiritual gifts and choosing to the body of Christ today. The selectivity is only in purpose and intent.

We all come by the blood of the spotless Lamb of God. The same blood avails for our sins that availed for the holy apostles. Therefore, we are moved by the same Holy Ghost.

God Is Only as Sovereign as His Word

We must begin with a certain amount of revelation in the Word of God. Then we pray the revealed Word of God. When we are done praying what we know or what comes to our understanding, we can pray in tongues. That is how the sovereignty of God works in working all things together for good. (See Romans 8:26–29.) God is only as sovereign as His Word. Psalm 132:8 says, "Thou hast magnified thy word above all thy Name." Isaiah 45:11 says, "Ask me of things to come concerning my sons, and concerning the work of my hands command ye me." We have a part to play in the working out and will of God.

God's Word is paramount to His operation, and through prayer and declaration we release His Word into the earth.

Authority in Two Realms?

Jesus said in the Great Commission of Mark 16, "All authority is given unto me, both in heaven and on earth. Go ye therefore and in my Name make disciples. I give unto you authority, to tread on serpents, and scorpions, and over all the power of the enemy."

We who receive the lordship of Christ and seek the kingdom of God have authority within our sphere of influence. David said, "The lines are fallen to me in pleasant places" (Psalm 16:6a). Where the righteous rule, there is peace. Satan has a lease with the unrenewed man of this world. This man must serve him through ignorance.

Even in man's natural unrenewed state, his created element is to rule the earth. The natural man has a certain amount of power in his will to resist Satan. This is because he was meant to dominate in the earth. Satan cannot trifle with someone who sets his will against him. He can only use deception. Having said that, we understand that all power is given unto us by our wonderful Lord Jesus.

The Devil is a usurper and an unlawful entity. The natural man still looks like God. That is why Satan tries so hard through ignorance, deceit, and rebellion to destroy him. Most persons willfully deny God by their selfish lifestyles, whereby Satan holds them under his delusion. The Devil has a terminal lease on the world and a system to keep it under his dominance. The reality is the earth and its fullness are the Lord's. God told Adam and Eve to have dominion. We were in them and are now redeemed through Christ, the second Adam.

As to the sovereignty of God, God says that He will do nothing except He first reveal it to his prophets (Amos 3:7). Where are the voices for this generation?

The whole issue of legal authority in prayer is unknown to most people. Somehow people believe Jesus is in heaven doing all the praying for us, so we don't really have to. If we do, though, he may give us extra points on rewards day. Is there any substance to this type of thinking?

Can Jesus Pray for Us in Heaven?

It is jurisdictionally impossible for Jesus to be praying for us in heaven. Perhaps we can begin to implore the saints in glory who have gone on before to grant us something from their realm?

It cannot be so. The two realms do not physically intersect. Jesus is in heaven, and we are on the earth. The Father has sent the Holy Spirit to us in efficacy of Christ. The Holy Spirit is on this earth to pray God's perfect will through us.

Jesus lives in heaven, where He "ever liveth to make intercession for the saints." He has made covenant with us. A covenant involves two parties, and each has a responsibility to uphold. He gave us a pattern for prayer. "Thy will be done on earth, as it is in heaven." We pray the will of God on earth. He releases it from heaven.

The only intersect between heaven and earth is the blood of Christ. This is the propitiation spoken of in 1 John 2:2 that ascends before the Father. Jesus' blood was shed on the earth for our redemption and applied to the mercy seat in heaven.

Jesus is our attorney. By conquest and position He has finished His work. He is seated in heaven until His enemies are made His footstool. This is becoming interesting. We are to be laborers together with Christ to enforce the victory He already has won. We are His mouth, hands, and feet in the earth. "Wherefore God hath highly exalted Him above every Name that is named." His name implores mercy on our behalf before the Father.

Jesus' work on earth is done. He is seated in heaven but sits in position as the High Priest over His church. Through the Holy Spirit, He is on earth interceding with that same mercy through the Spirit-filled believer.

If the believer does not pray, Jesus cannot intercede for us on earth. There is no other way to receive the promises. Just as God has concluded all under sin, so salvation is all-inclusive "not willing that any should perish" (John 3:16). It is the individual's responsibility to receive.

We must pray for the unbeliever. God has poured out His Spirit on all unbelievers as well as believers. The preaching of the gospel is significant to hearing. We must reach them with the mercy of God through preaching and prayer, binding the Devil from them. We must claim them for God and loosen them from the Devil's grip of blindness and deception.

While Jesus was on earth, He had authority in His physical body. Now He sits at the right hand of God but has delegated that authority to His body on earth. He is waiting for us to accomplish the task on earth "till His enemies are made His footstool."

He is waiting for the manifestation of the sons of God. That is us. We are to be as Christ in the earth. As He is, so are we in this world. He is the firstborn of many brethren. We are begotten of the Father. He was the first begotten of the Father.

Some would say this is an amazing heretical error. It is so, only because it is so incredulous that we can be as Christ in the earth, doing the same miracles, accomplishing the same works.

How are we to know then, how to pray? It is in the book of the blood covenant, the Bible, where the will of God is revealed. Romans 8:26–28 says, "Likewise the Spirit helpeth us in our infirmities, when we know not how to pray, the Spirit Himself maketh intercession for us with groanings that cannot be uttered… and we know that all things work together for good to those who love God, for those who are called according to His purpose." We pray according to His Word as well as the Holy Spirit interceding for and through us.

How can the Holy Spirit pray for us in the earth? He must be embodied by the saints. We are His temple. We have this treasure in earthen vessels that the excellency of the power may be of God and not of ourselves. The Holy Spirit lives inside of us and helps us. The Holy Spirit in this passage is praying through us with inarticulate speech (tongues). This is what some persons have called a heavenly language. I am not sure it is so much heavenly but rather a kingdom language and a kingdom key in effecting the will and purposes of the King.

The King of glory is calling for sons of the kingdom to carry His authority into the earth. This kingdom has a new authority and comes with a language as well as a name to establish its borders. Part of establishing the kingdom of God is speaking in a language the Devil understands. Our part in praying the perfect will of God is limited by our understanding. That is why we pray through our unique prayer language in tongues as the Holy Spirit helps us. Engaging our tongues by faith is part of establishing the reign of God. Satan is dispossessed. The earth and its fullness are the Lord's. It is up to us to implement that authority through faith-filled words, prayer with understanding, and praying in tongues.

That is how Jesus prays for us. If we will not pray, He cannot pray for us. Jesus is in heaven standing in that place of intercession. The Holy Spirit never speaks on His own behalf but always exalts Jesus. Jesus is the one praying for us through the Holy Spirit, utilizing our renewed minds, our submitted wills, and our tongues. If we abide in Christ, He will send us more of His Holy Spirit to enable us to pray more effectively.

As we pray in the Holy Ghost, we then do the will of the Father. As we abide in Him, He abides in us, and the Father will love Him and be a Father to us. Whatsoever we ask the Father in Jesus's name, He will do it (Mark 11:24).

CHAPTER 9

MILITANT PRAYER: DELIVER US FROM EVIL

Big Demons on the Roof

I have heard a demon manifest on the roof of my house when I entertained a lustful element through idolatry. It sounded like a five-hundred-pound man tromping on the roof. We must believe that once we have been enlightened, we cannot turn back from God. The Enemy does not give us a break.

Other times I have smelled death. Sometimes when evil spirits are present, there is a pervading odor.

The Blast of His Nostrils

Psalm 18:15–17 talks about the power the Lord uses in bringing deliverance to the afflicted. "At thy rebuke, O Lord, at the blast of the breath of thy nostrils; He sent from above, he took me; he drew me out of many waters; He delivered me from my strong enemy." The following story helps to illustrate this principle.

He Grabbed His Chest and Fell to the Floor

Dealing with the Devil is a spiritual work. I can relate an instance concerning this subject when the power of God came to deliver a man some years ago. It was at a men's prayer meeting in one of the fellow's basements.

A very handsome man was there who had a rather prolific past. He was a new convert. He was—or he had been—a male prostitute. He was still addicted to cocaine and bound in that lifestyle.

With no real knowledge of anything, we prayed in a circle. The leader prayed a nice prayer for all of us as we held hands in signified solidarity. When he was done, I said to him that I felt we were not done yet. He kind of wasn't sure about me telling him that because he was the leader, but I persisted.

We prayed again in the spirit (tongues). The Spirit of God moved me to blare out like a riled moose—not a roar but almost like I was blasting through something. This young man grabbed his chest and fell to the floor like he had been knocked out by the Holy Spirit.

I believe a lot of demons got evicted that evening with just one spiritual encounter and confrontation. He was drawn to me afterward. That is where counseling and further prayer may have been helpful. He needed to repair the brokenness and misguided attachments and be filled with the Father's love.

Is Satan to Be Feared?

If we were to say that Satan is to be feared, many Christians would agree. This is only because of their ignorance of spiritual conquest. It is all about our position in Christ. We have overcome him because greater is He that is in us than he that is in the world.

Dealing with the Devil is ugly. If the voice of the Lord empowers us with a roar against the Devil, he has to go. He is a trespasser and a usurper. He is unclean and ugly.

That is the dirty business of warfare. We cut him down. We stretch out the sword of the Lord against him. Every spirit that does not honor the name and the blood of the Lord Jesus Christ must come to attention. If they have no grounds of occupation, they must leave.

The Word of God releases people from his grip. That is why good preaching is so essential. It is also the application and the confrontation. Enemy spirits don't just leave. They must be confronted. This is how Jesus demonstrated His power over evil spirits. Commanding prayer is standing in the place of Jesus and taking authority over the evil spirit in His name.

James 4:7 says that we must submit to the Lord and then resist the Devil. Only then will he flee from you. If he has a well-entrenched program in one's life, though, he will need to be evicted. This is the work of the Holy Spirit. In being released from demons, we must be available to initiate the process. Then God works.

It is the Lord who by His eternal Spirit manifests His power through us. That is what gets the job done. He has revealed Himself through His Word. Now we must receive the application. That is what releases the manifestation.

Jesus said that we need to pray after this manner in the Lord's Prayer. "Thy will be done on earth, as it is in heaven." We command on earth, and Jesus commands in heaven. What we bind on earth, heaven binds. What we loose on earth, heaven looses.

Joseph Schellenberg, D.C.C.

All Called to Prayer, Not All Called to the Office of Prayer

Intercession is seldom recognized as a special ministry because prayer is a part of our stewardship as Christians. Engaging the same argument, we could say that evangelizing, shepherding, prophesying, or teaching all are part of our Christian stewardship. Then how are some called to special offices in these same areas as outlined in Ephesians 4:11?

Why is it that the most vocal opposition to this type of thinking comes from leaders in offices who often flow in powerful gifts themselves? They have great oratorical skills and verbal fluency, called to offices such as the prophet, preacher, evangelist or teacher. These are those with distinction in the church. They have a rationalistic mindset, employing and teaching leadership strategies, yet have little understanding of this dimension in the Spirit.

There is a specific ministry of intercession and deliverance to deal with the Devil. This could be categorized under spiritual gifts with manifestations in the area of the utterance gifts. This gift operates with specialty in the diversities of tongues. The gifts of revelation, word of knowledge, and word of wisdom may also play some part in releasing an authoritative command.

All are called to pray. All have power over the Devil, but not all are as effective in bringing down spiritual wickedness in high places. Higher level spiritual warfare is not of human origin. As we engage our will, set ourselves to seek the Lord in this area, and persist, the Holy Spirit will engage us in warfare.

All are empowered against the Devil, but not all are as effective. That is not to say that even the weakest member in the body of Christ does not have the same power as the most prominent.

To some degree it has to do with gift, design, and strategy. If one gives themselves into an area and is desirous, we can grow into an area. God honors our faith. Some, though, have greater gifting and entrance into the spirit realm in a particular area. He gives gifts to each severally as He wills.

This may be where the sovereignty of God can be applied. We may see that one has greater entrance and impact in this realm. Gifts and calling may involve God's own choosing. However, we are to grow great and desire greater gifts, effectiveness, and influence.

Most persons have not learned or perceived that a real power experience in spiritual warfare can be quite fun. But one has to set him or herself to the task and get into motion and then persevere until the breakthrough comes.

The apostle Paul said that we need to desire earnestly the best gifts. He was referring to prophecy, but we can desire and grow in our capacity to be used in other areas as well.

Paul followed this admonition with the love chapter. He is putting it all into perspective. He really is saying, "You may feel like you have great power in your gifting," even as the disciples were amazed at the power to cast out demons.

So we ought not to be glamorized in our ability to flow in a gift given to us by the Holy Spirit. It is still primarily about relationship—relationship to God in heaven and to the people on earth.

Our ability to war is temporal. Relationships are eternal. That is not to say that we take our job lightly, as we are in essence contending for the kingdom of God. We must do things God's way. He is doing His thing through us. If He wants to have people falling all over chairs, laughing uproariously, or if He wants to shake the ecclesiastical guardians out of religious piety, that is His prerogative.

CHAPTER 10
OTHER MANIFESTATIONS, OUTPOURINGS, AND THE VOICE OF THE LORD

Spiritual Shaking

When people shake, there is a transitioning from flesh to spirit. There is something spiritual happening—a transference of spiritual power or entity. This in itself is neither good nor evil. When soul ties are made, one can usually go back to an experience where there was a spiritual transference from one individual to another. When one is filled with the Holy Spirit, many times he or she will feel a quivering.

Shaking can go both ways, where it is also seen to be the reverse. When one is offering his or her soul to an idol (usually through sexual activity or drugs), a demon can enter, and that person will shake under the power as well.

But we are of God, and the demons must leave. When people shake under God's power, strongholds are shattered, the Enemy is expelled, and God is able by His Holy Spirit to fill those areas.

It is of interest that in a deliverance one of the commands we give is for the demon to come from every part of this person's body.

We still offer up some parts of our bodies to idols. Others have been held back through self-protection.

When one has been wounded, abused, or traumatized as a child, many times there are areas even closed to our knowledge. Sometimes a blocking demon has attached itself to the infraction, keeping us from remembering what happened or feeling anything related to the intrusion. This keeps one in a developmentally arrested condition to the pain and the trauma.

Dr. Paul Hegstrom (Author of Broken Children, Grown-Up Pain) says children do not yet have the necessary chemicals in their brains to reason things out. This process begins at puberty. The child is still in the age of directives, and he or she processes everything to reaction in trauma. They may continue to blame themselves, or they may not know why they react the way they do. This is why the Devil seeks to damage children. Then they are held captive for a lifetime.

We must be willing at some time to open those areas up to God, no matter how painful they are. They may need to be reprocessed through Spirit-led counseling. Only then can God come in and fill them with His love and healing.

When God comes to visit, people become intoxicated with His presence. People may fall under His power, getting up and stumble around in a drunken state of spiritual euphoria. He can do that. After all, God is the most attractive and beautiful encounter we will ever have. Jesus' robe glistened with the glory on the mount. Moses' face glowed. The disciples along the road to Emmaus burned in their hearts. We may also have our own senses stirred.

This may give some clue as to why a move of God, such as the ministry under Rodney Howard Browne or the Toronto Blessing, came to be.

Joseph Schellenberg, D.C.C.

How Does an Outpouring such as the Toronto Blessing Begin?

Let us consider some possibilities. It is possible some persons are easily stirred in their emotions and are looking for a stimulant to attach themselves to. They have a level of habituation and are looking for new, more extreme, and more bizarre activity to stimulate their dopamine levels. Some persons may have found religious ecstasy or may be caught up in a pursuit of adrenaline or perpetual excitement. I have seen this characteristic with some persons in the twenty-seven-hour burn (a continuous worship experience staged in Calgary). This assumption, though, rather excludes God from the equation.

If God is totally sovereign, could it be He just decided it was time to act? When it is on God's timetable, He decides what and when. It is just like the return of Christ… somewhat of a mystery… be ready. I think God desires us to be a part of His timing.

It is said that the outpouring of the Spirit at Airport Vineyard was a complete surprise and an unexpected move of God. James Beverly talks about the message Randy Clark presented the night it began. Clark gave a dramatic account of his own experience and manifestations under the ministry of Rodney Howard-Browne. When Clark extended the invitation for ministry that night, the people's expectation was for the same.

Although faith is preached, expectation does play a part in releasing the manifestation. Paul said the Lord confirmed his preaching with signs and wonders following. That may be one answer.

It is also a biblical truth that anointing or power is usually caught by being present in an anointed service or transferred through the laying on of hands. To illustrate, Elisha received the double portion anointing of Elijah. The spirit of Moses was put on Joshua as well as upon the seventy delegated leaders. Paul and the presbytery laid their hands on Timothy for an impartation. Even the doctrine of the "laying on of hands" for impartation is part of the Great Commission in Mark 16.

Another response might be that Toronto is the most ethically diverse city on the planet. People have conjectured that God is reenacting the Pentecostal experience of the book of Acts, touching this age as He did with diverse nations in the first century.

Although the world has felt the influence of this revival, I feel there is a greater element involved.

I would like to think that God has rewarded the hungry as well as the prayers of intercessors of nations with an outpouring of His Holy Spirit. The revival then continues to break through local regions with focused influence and territorial reign. Part of that intercession involves warfare and spiritual enactment as are seen in the spiritual confrontations with local despots or rulers of darkness. This explosion of spiritual intercession releases the glory of God in fuller measure.

These manifestations are not an end in themselves. Nor are they for the purpose of worship. They are rather empowered by the Holy Spirit for the rooting out and removal of enemy infiltration.

A Direct Tongue to Deal with the Devil

The Spirit gives life to the Word, but there is a direct tongue to deal with the Devil in spiritual intercession. When the Holy Ghost intercedes through us with a militant tongue (see Romans 8:26), there is direct confrontation with demonic spirits and rulers of darkness. This may be what contributes to some of the misunderstanding. People see only the visible natural and sensory data. They may attribute some natural psychology, trying to figure out what the gestures, roaring, barking, or tongues may be all about. This may look like chaotic frenzy, but there is a spiritual parallel and reality.

This is an exercise in militant warfare. People are availing themselves to be used as spiritual intercessors, snatching power away from the kingdoms of this world. "The kingdoms of this world are become the Kingdom of our God"

(see Revelation 11). There is an exchange of power, rule, and authority.

This begins on a local level. We govern ourselves, our families, our churches, and our countries. We are to seek first the kingdom of God. That means we must restore what the Enemy has stolen from us.

This type of warfare will make available a greater capacity to love the unlovely. It will also restore unity in the church. The world will recognize us when we can get into agreement and love one another as Christ loves the church.

The gift of intercessory prayer works in conjunction with the Word. A direct engagement and confrontation of the Enemy involves both a militant tongue and strong preaching of the gospel.

The Voice of the Lord

Not every person has a developed and strong militant tongue that the Devil understands. The voice of the Lord is powerful. He may inspire us to roar against the Enemy. That does not mean prophesy. That means to roar. Prophecy has its place, but when God empowers a roar, kingdoms are shaken.

The roar of the Spirit has come upon me in powerful manifestation. I could only describe it as something like a fire-breathing dragon that pushes back hordes of demonic hosts. The roar of the Lord is powerful.

We cannot discount manifestations unless they are of the flesh. When God gives a tongue, it has meaning. When God gives a voice, it carries strength. When God thunders, the mountains tremble. We must begin to see the spiritual connection.

When we travail, it may sound like we are giving birth. This is not a physical birth but the physical act of travailing. This manifestation is birthed in the womb of the spiritual. It must be involved in carrying out the spiritual.

God is a spirit yet has joyfully allowed us as physical beings to enter into the spiritual. He not only wants us but has actually made it so that He needs us. He needs our bodies to birth the spiritual. We are His temple. We must become devoted to Him, a living sacrifice that He can pour Himself through.

We are the only vessel He can work through in this earth. To discount his operations would mean to doubt the voice of our spirits where he dwells. We can grow in this area. Not everyone receives 100 percent accuracy every time. Some experimentation needs to be recognized. We are becoming spiritual. We are born all tipped upside down. God desires to be back in control where our spirits begin to dictate our movements.

We are to test the spirits with His Word. John gives us the criteria. Every spirit that denies that Jesus is the Christ is from the world. A spirit against Christ cannot confess the Lordship of Christ.

When I go into areas I am not familiar with, I confess the ownership of Christ that I am bought by His precious blood. I know His voice, and He knows me. That happens a lot when one is navigating unchartered waters. We have the Word, but all our experiences are not necessarily documented. We just have to test our spirits when we begin to go into areas of warfare.

At various times a demon may speak through you for the purpose of identification and location, and we may cast him out. That is a bit confusing at first, but that is the nature of deliverance.

That is how God communicates with us—through His Word, through our renewed minds, and through the intuition of a reborn human spirit. We must learn to recognize the strength of His voice through our times of prayer and devotion to Him.

The Spirit of Man Is the Candle of the Lord

When we speak in tongues, the voice of the Lord comes from the hidden man of the heart. It is through him that we receive unction and utterance. The spirit of man is the "candle of the Lord, searching all the inward parts of the belly" (Proverbs 20:27).

If the Enemy's voice comes to us, it is from without, not within. The only confusion exists when our own spirits begin to interpret something through our emotions. Our soul (mind, will, and emotions) has a voice, but it must be renewed to the Word of God. We get used to hearing God's voice just like children know their fathers or mothers' voices.

Prophecy or interpreting our prayers works in a similar manner. The implementation of the physical organ must be submitted to the spirit of man, which is where the unction begins. This may begin with an inarticulate language; it is ciphered, then decrypted through a renewed mind and formed. Depending on how well one's engine is tuned, interpretation involves some subjectivity. Using every facet of one's creative mind and cognition, words are formed that have their origin in the spirit.

This is where every different kind of spiritual utterance must come from. It does not originate from the mind but enters the mind from the spirit. A renewed mind can stir up the spirit. Paul said to Timothy to "stir up the gift within you." This is what a renewed mind will do. It can get the engine started.

Sometimes we don't feel like praying, or there seems to be no unction. A renewed mind can begin to pray according to knowledge and revealed will.

The process can be like a small engine starting a larger engine. When the spirit becomes engaged, the mind becomes utilized in releasing greater unction.

CHAPTER 11

ONE CANNOT LEAD WHERE ONE HAS NEVER GONE

The Leaders in Our Churches and Bible Schools for the Most Part Have Never Been to the School of the Supernatural.

I was at a soaker meeting where a Bible school team was to minister. The leader appeared very interested in entering into the Spirit through worship with an inspired DVD. He had all the right words. He had a little dance that he shuffled around with. He looked very cool! I was in a great spirit of expectancy.

The reality was that he had never been to the school of the supernatural, so he could not take us there. He just enjoyed the preeminence of the show and hearing himself speak. Then he wanted to lay hands on all the women with an emotional vulnerability in order to put himself into admiration.

He did not like me at all. I really had no idea till I opened my eyes. He was standing right beside me, basically physically intimidating me so that I would not enter into prayer or any of the utterance gifts.

I have often had this kind of thing happen, and I have wondered why my spirit is shut down. It was not my mind that was catching on right away; however, my spirit was grieved, and I was closed down.

People cannot lead you to where they have never gone. Ministry leaders esteem the admiration of men higher than their hunger for God. Rational expressions of faith along with emotionally driven programs prevail.

It may be that leaders fear a loss of control will reflect on their reputations. It is also possible that they are just there for the position. Where there is no knowledge, there can be no receiving or entering. Unless people are really desperate for God, they will never dare to enter into unfamiliar areas.

This forming of tradition is not only in denominational circles but in present-day Pentecostalism. Ministers have heard how to do it. They use all the right clichés so that one thinks, *Yes, I finally found a place that can enter in to the depths of God*, only to be very quickly shut down.

New expressions in worship have taken the initiative where churches are beginning to have artistic spiritual expressions through painting; others are in costumes dancing and waving flags.

Who will lead us into the supernatural? That is not to say creative expressions have no validity in worship, but we supplant the real gifts of the spirit with the programs of man.

We have to be so in charge of everything. Is not the Spirit of God capable of leading His own services? Why is it that every leader wants to be so in charge. Can they not just sit down and minister to the Lord, or must the spectators have another theatrical experience.

When hungry people begin to let God lead, He will bring us into authenticity.

CHAPTER 12

MUSIC AND WORSHIP IN THE MODERN WORLD

New songs and styles of worship are a part of new revelation and revival. We need to minister to the Lord in song. He will release new desire and inspiration to enter His glory.

If we ever take a camping trip and sleep beside a marsh in a tent, we are almost overwhelmed by the incredible amount of noises the created organisms of God's earth are making. All of creation is offering praises up to God, and He loves it.

Musical Snoring and Croaking

It was deep in the night. I was sleeping in a tent with all the frogs and crickets out there, and they were all busy offering up their praises to God. I had been told on one occasion that I snored in sync with nature. I would snore, and the frog would croak in synchronization. I would snore, and the frog would croak in double unison. This was a peculiar phenomenon. Even creation has a rhythm in worship. We are all part of its order.

Another time when I snored, it was told me later, I was singing. I was making musical melodies in song while I was snoring. Our spirit is alive to God in expression even when we sleep.

Song of Solomon 5:2 says, "I sleep, but my heart waketh." Some have been awakened to find themselves praying in tongues even while they were sleeping because praying in tongues leaves one's mind free to do other things like rest!

Jesus said that even the rocks would cry out because of our inability or inadequate expression of worship. It is so evident why we need a stronger, more fluid language of worship through tongues.

Acts 2 has recorded the first experience of the Spirit's outpouring. In Acts 2:11, we read that the people heard them speak in their own tongues the wonderful works of God.

Heaven had a chief worshipper with all the instruments of an orchestra built into him. His name was Lucifer, "son of the morning." He was clothed in glory but fell to the earth. Into him were built the "noise of thy viols, pipes and tabrets."

These are the three primary musical sections of an orchestra—strings, wind, and percussion. Ezekiel 28:13b–14a says, "The workmanship of thy tabrets and of thy pipes was prepared in thee in the day that thou wast created. Thou art the anointed cherub that covereth." Isaiah 14:11 says, "The noise of thy viols:" Isaiah goes on to lament, "How art thou fallen from heaven, O Lucifer, son of the morning… yet thou shalt be brought down to hell, to the sides of the pit. They that see thee shall narrowly look upon thee, and consider the saying, Is this the man that made the earth to tremble, that did shake kingdoms?"

We must realize the awesome power of the anointing through music. David demonstrated this by playing his harp for Saul. When he played, the evil spirit left Saul. Holy Spirit-anointed music scares the Devil.

The Key Is the Anointing

The key to worship is the anointing. The anointing is the tangible presence of God. People in nominal churches don't believe in the tangibility of God's power. They spiritualize everything. The Devil just winks.

But we are of those who believe the gospel is the power of God. Paul said, "I pray that your whole body, soul and spirit be preserved unto the day of Jesus Christ."

Jesus said, "The Spirit of God has anointed me to preach the gospel to the poor, to heal the sick, to mend the brokenhearted; and to preach deliverance to the captives; recovery of sight to the blind; to set at liberty them that are bruised; to preach the favourable year of the Lord" (Luke 4:18). It was said of Jesus that He went about doing good and healing all that were oppressed by the Devil.

The anointing started with telling the poor that they didn't have to be poor anymore and telling those bound with afflictions that they need not suffer anymore. The bruised were those who suffered infractions, betrayal, and losses, people carrying deep inner wounds. These did not have to carry the painful memories any longer, but the healing balm of Gilead would anoint and heal them. Jesus would also anoint their eyes with eye salve so that they could see the real picture, namely that Jesus loves them unconditionally and is able to restore and replace what for a whole lifetime was lost.

The Devil is afraid of the blood of Jesus because it blinds Him, sending confusion into his camp. The compulsive addict is freed from a lifetime of bondage.

The anointing is Jesus, who is the treasure that we carry inside. The anointing overflows on the outside like a balm upon us. It is a fragrance that we carry. To some it restores life, and to others it brings conviction for sin to repentance (see 2 Corinthians 2:16).

Many times it is through the gifts we carry that the anointing operates. It may be a word that we speak that can be anointed. The laying on of hands in Mark 16:18 was part of the Great Commission. As we pray and lay hands on people, a transference of the anointing occurs. The sick are healed.

We may sing songs in church. They carry emotional sentiment like a birthday card or a card of thanks. You open it, read it, and smile. Then you close it and put it in your attic. It has no substance.

Satan understands the anointing. His music fills the earth with his anointing. People under his spell commit murders, kill themselves, and carry out perverted and lustful desires. He possesses them with his anointing. He may enter them through the narcotics of sound and sexual stimuli in strip clubs and bars.

The Devil is very interested in the music ministry. He desires to captivate young people who are gifted and groomed for the kingdom of God. Through worldly allurement and promise of power, they become his emissaries. These carry out his plans to invade and possess millions of our youth in every culture.

Musical instruments are created elements of physics. The oscillation of air through a column, whether generated through a pipe, a human voice, tone generator, or string on a sounding board, can be an instrument utilized for good or evil. I have played some of the most amazing organs in churches and cathedrals. They are used in extolling the glory and majesty of God.

Music may carry an atmosphere of warmth, peace, jubilance, or sadness. It can be used for oppression or violence. It may either carry heavenly strains of glory and release angels or be generic and have little spiritual significance. It may be offered to the Devil with a satanic anointing for demons to work. Suicide many times is conspired through music and lyrics.

Music is the most powerful thing in the universe. In its design and origin it is made to bring worship to God. God fills it with Himself. Heaven is permeated with music. Music sets an atmosphere where the gospel can be preached under the anointing of the Spirit of God. The Devil knows that, and it terrorizes him.

Satan wants all the attention. He is after the glory and the anointing. Every bar is filled with his music. There is no spiritual vacuum.

Music, whether rock 'n' roll or whatever style, has always been a target for the critics. The legalists and the gullible seek to program God through their own lenses. That way things don't get out of hand. They want people to stay in their controlled environments but never really reach anyone outside of their circles.

A strictly legal mind tends to bypass heart issues. The greatest law is one that uncovers hidden motives and intents. A correct understanding of scripture will divide soul and spirit and will discern the thoughts and intents of the heart. Music penetrates the soul, allowing the Word to penetrate the heart.

Paul said that as ministers, we were not sufficient in ourselves, or to think anything of ourselves, but rather our sufficiency is of God "who hath made us able ministers of the new testament; not of the letter, but of the spirit: for the letter killeth, but the spirit giveth life" (2 Corinthians 3:6).

We must be musicians attuned to the Spirit of God, skillful in instrumentation and voice as well as inspiration, prophetic insight, and the gifts of revelation.

Supernatural Spiritual Songs

I used to go to a native reserve north of Winnipeg for services on Sunday afternoons. There I would play music. A few times I went to their Bible study during the week.

I was leading it one time, and during the prayer time the Lord gave me the most beautiful spiritual song I had ever heard. I could not have dreamed it up. It was totally under strong inspiration of the Spirit. The Lord was singing over us the most beautiful song, the song of the Lord.

Aboriginal Cultures More Accepting of Spiritual Experiences

Culturally native North Americans attribute more phenomenon to spirituality than white persons. This has made them more receptive to the supernatural but also more vulnerable. We understand that the Devil works primarily through the sensory realm. We must realize that there is a supernatural element in dealing with the Devil.

God has transcended the natural through the gifts of the Holy Spirit. This is the third grouping of manifestations—the utterance gifts as well as the power gifts. That is why the Devil wants them attributed to him. They do him incredible damage. Tongues and the utterance gifts have been the most divisive topic in the church. We need to restore them to the church.

We need to recognize the limitations of our cultural heritage in relation to the spiritual. Some of that is gaining maturity in the self-life, recognizing that the emotional realm is distinct from the spiritual.

Methods of dealing with strongholds have a subjective element. This is why we develop our spirits and become less afraid of moving into untrodden territory. We must have a strong scriptural basis for our lives in yielding up the self-life.

We realize that although we have a different cultural heritage, we sing the same redemptive song, the song of the redeemed.

We have the same Word of God. It is also the same blood of our Savior, the Lord Jesus Christ, that adopts us into His family. He gives us the same precious gift of the Holy Spirit to seal us for redemption.

It is this same power that raised Christ from the dead and allows us to bind and loosen the grip of Satan off of our lives.

Be Renewed in the Spirit of Your Mind

A new song will come from a renewed heart and mind. It may sometimes be a prophetic word or just comforting and reassuring.

We must be renewed in the spirits of our minds. The mind is an unrenewed member just like our flesh. Peter said that we need to repent and *be converted*. It was a process. We are admonished to not be conformed to this world but be transformed by this renewal of our minds. In so speaking, the voice of the Lord must come from our spirits and be de-ciphered through renewed minds.

Interestingly enough, interpreting our tongues does not initially involve our renewed minds. It is learning to recognize syllables and receiving them by faith. Sometimes our minds help to put them together, but there is a subjective learned element to interpretation.

Paul said of he who speaks in an unknown tongue, "Let him pray that he may interpret." This area requires some experimentation in our personal prayer language in order to experience it and grow in the gift.

The song of the Lord may come because He longs to commune with us and bless us. He longs for us to be filled to overflowing. Jesus compared us to old wineskins that have become inflexible and unable to expand in capacity to receive His Spirit.

It may be that a tangible experience with God would open up our spirits to receive more songs and prophetic insight. This may be why some people are slain in the spirit when they come in contact with the anointing. God longs to give more of Himself to them, yet their perception of Him has limited them.

Moses said, "Why do you limit the Holy One of Israel?" God longed to provide and manifest His glory to them, yet they constantly rebelled in their hearts and turned to idols.

Have we really learned to recognize the yearning of the Father for His children? Jesus understood that love. That is why He prayed for us in John 17 so that we were able to share in the relationship of love that He had with His Father. He wanted us to be family.

A renewed mind must encompass new boundaries for identity and family. We have an earthly family and heritage. Jesus is calling us to larger communion and responsibility. We need to feel the yearning of our Father God and the Holy Spirit, the earnestness of our inheritance.

He comes to give us a new song, and He has named us with His name "of whom the whole family of heaven and earth are named" (Ephesians 3:15).

CHAPTER 13

THE ROAR OF THE LORD

Roaring with Big Ushers

One time my family was in Edmonton during the summer camp meeting where numerous speakers would come together for a weeklong revival. We made it our practice every year to go there as part of our family holidays.

This particular night Ellen Parsley (mother and intercessor for Rod) was ministering. She was not particularly interesting, somewhat hard to listen to, so I went to the washroom for a break.

Upon returning from my break, Parsley was beginning to do personal altar ministry. I was sitting right at the back, and all of a sudden I had this huge unction to roar. I fought it with my mind. I said to myself, *Here are several thousand people with really big ushers.* (In reality they were security officers, all of them instructed in martial arts.) *I do not want to be sat on and have the Devil cast out of me.* So I reasoned it away. This powerful unction came to me three times. Then it left.

It is of interest that many times when God speaks in a certain way, He will speak three times. Peter experienced this with the voice on the rooftop in Acts 11:10.

During this time Ellen started into the audience, her team of catchers trying to keep up. There were people being slain in the spirit and being flung all over chairs. It was pandemonium.

It was not a minute later that the speaker said, "There is a roar in the Spirit. Let's everyone roar." Well, that was a roar but conjured in the flesh. The Holy Ghost had anointed me to roar, and I held back. It grieved me that I was so concerned about what people would think rather than obeying God.

Preservice Intercession

I remember one particular roar that was Spirit-empowered. I used to be involved in preservice intercession in a small room off to the side. Most people would just come and pray fairly predictable prayers. I usually wanted to wait for the movement of the Holy Spirit.

The silence sometimes made the people a bit uncomfortable. I guess, if I was to lead, then it appeared like I wasn't leading and maybe I was waiting for someone else to lead. How is it that we know how to conduct every prayer meeting after our great knowledge and wisdom?

One particular time—it may have been the last time I was in the lead in the prayer room—I had this amazingly powerful roar. It was as if I were a fire-breathing dragon blowing or pushing back all the hordes of demons from hell. Psalm 97:3 says, "A fire goes before him, and burneth up his enemies round about."

I am not sure if words can explain the feeling or unction. The pastor had been in the building, and I guess that sent him for a spin. That was the last time I roared in his church.

I am saying that true spiritual warfare is spiritual. When we get involved with our ability to reason everything, we stay in the sense realm. That is where everything is done decently and in order—men's order but not God's order.

The roar of the Lord is not something to take lightly. The Lord does roar against His enemies. He empowers the roar but needs our voice. To metaphysically speak about a roar is to miss the greatest joy of conquest. God wants us to be conquerors together with Christ.

It is like a man in a bulldozer. One lever gives him tremendous power. We are conquerors with Christ. God is inviting us to sit with Him in heavenly places and do enemy infiltration and sabotage. We are seated with Him. He is doing the driving but directing us through militant tongues and voices to dispel the Enemy. The voice of the Lord is clothed in majesty. It is He that rules in and through us.

Jesus prayed in John 17 that we would be in Him, as He is in the Father. Together He would make His abode in us, and He would come to us. We are His, and He is ours. We abide in Him, and whatever we ask, we have the petitions desired of Him. That is Holy Communion. That is why we must be holy, as He is holy.

This communion goes both ways. When He desires to move through us with a Spirit-empowered utterance, we must be ready. God desires to move through us in power.

It is not power, though, that characterizes the children of God. It is glory, and the purpose of the glory is that the church may be one. Then the world will believe that Jesus came from God (see John 17:22–23). It is through unity (and love) that the world will recognize us. It is through the glory that they (the church) will be made perfect in one even as Jesus and the Father are one.

Just as intercession through the Spirit moves us into militant prayer, our communion with the Father moves us into compassion and love for the brethren. First John 4:20 says, "If a man say, I love God and hateth his brother, he is a liar, for he that loveth not his brother whom he hath seen, how can he love God whom he hath not seen." That is a double imperative. We are not even close to God if we do not love our brothers. So the new move of God will be characterized by both power and love.

CHAPTER 14

THE CHURCH AND ONE'S PERSONAL DEVOTION TO GOD

All the believer's strength must begin in the quiet place, in the garden with God. It is said that Adam walked with God in the cool of the garden. Adam wasn't totally as relational as Eve when it came to talking. (This may be why God decided to make Eve.)

Adam and Eve

It seems that even Adam was a bit crude with the fellowship God intended. Maybe he was just like most guys, caught up in the world of images, objects, and recreational companionship. Maybe God wanted to talk to him about deeper things than his job of naming all the animals.

As it came about, God decided He needed someone who was more interested in talking about relationships than animals. That is why He made Eve. Well, that went much better with the three of them, but still something was missing from Adam. God had breathed the breath (*ruauh* in Hebrew, meaning "breath in motion") of life into him, but perhaps he wasn't developed spiritually to his potential.

That is why still today the second most important need for men in marriage relationships is for recreational companionship. Adam just wanted to talk to God about his job, about all the neat animals that God had given him to name, and about his garden. Eve needed relationship. So did God, but God loved them both so much. He still covered them with the blood of animal skins after they sinned so that they could be redeemed.

I have used a bit of folly in relating the Genesis account, but am calling men to attention. We have left our call to leadership in the home and in the church. It has cost us in that most of our church services are emotionally driven, and our kids are a little too tied to Mama.

The Church: A Verbal Experience

New findings in *Positive Psychology* report that women have 11 percent more neurons governing language and hearing than men do. The principle hub of both emotion and memory formation in the brain (the hippocampus) is larger in the female brain than in men. This is true also of brain circuitry relating to language and observing emotion. The corpus callosum is larger in women better facilitating the action of language and response. Tests have shown that women outperform men by huge margins in verbal fluency. They use more of their brains during speech, making themselves better at expressing themselves verbally.

The church is built on this principle. The church has become an almost entirely verbal experience. Words are in the bulletin, hymnals, readings and prayers. Sermon notes accompany the lecture style sermon. Women are taking notes for discussion over the dinner table.

Christianity exhibits little active learning, but is big on verbal listening. University studies have shown that a memorized long uninterrupted monologue is an ineffective way of teaching people anything. Men especially have difficulty with sermons, as they use one side of their brain to comprehend and the other side to respond emotionally.

Paul comments on the significance of anointed preaching in the sharing of the gospel with signs following. There should be gifts of healing or miracles, gifts of revelation, a word of knowledge or prophetic insight, wisdom, or a sign with tongues and interpretation; these should accompany and be the natural outworking of the message.

Dry Sermons

Earlier I alluded to the fact that perhaps God was tired of dry sermons in His church. Perhaps that is the reason He would have starched men of the cloth totally undone. (*See Great Awakening 2014 Rodney Howard Browne Meetings, You Tube.com.*) Someone would try to give a message but were so under the anointing that they could only laugh uproariously. Maybe that is God's answer to our religiosity. We are not really entering into all that He has for us in the church. When the church begins to be filled with his glory, there will be great favor upon the people of God, and many will come to Christ (Acts 2–4)

There is no other generation that has the ability and joy of experiencing relationship in conquest over the Enemy as we do. We have entered into the frontlines of spiritual warfare. We have Jesus, who has gone before us, His blood, His Word, and His name.

We have the power to snatch souls from death. We can either live in our comfortable seats in church or sacrifice some of our recreational pursuits for prayer and the purpose of seeking God.

Having devotions means devoting time to God. It means setting aside a particular place and time for God. Jesus went to a certain place. Sometimes He would spend the whole night in the Mount of Olives. The disciples were in their certain place, the upper room. The certain place is where we go, and regularly meet with God. That place gets into us, to where; when we are there, God is there.

We have missed that element of reverence for a certain place in our churches. "Let us serve God with reverence and godly fear, for our God is a consuming fire" (Hebrews 12:28). We come into the house of worship so casually. When we enter for certain times, there ought to be a holy atmosphere.

Then we ought to pray after the manner that Jesus taught His disciples. This was a model or pattern to follow. He did not say, "Pray this word for word." He was giving us a formula for the Holy Ghost to follow. The Holy Spirit needs something to work with.

Moreover, there needs to be structure in the church before the Holy Spirit can fill it. After Solomon's temple was completed, the glory came and filled it "so that the priests could not stand to minister" (2Chronicles 5:14).

CHAPTER 15

PRAYER WITH THE UNDERSTANDING

After This Manner Pray Ye

Jesus gave a directive in the form of a pattern for us to follow in our personal devotion to God.

He begins His discourse in prayer with this: "After this manner pray ye: Our Father which art in heaven; Hallowed be thy Name."

That is worship. We begin to worship Him for who He is. He is precious. He is wonderful. His name reveals His nature and perfection. His name gives you power and attorney. We are thankful for what He has done, but we worship Him for who He is.

We can rehearse the names of God. "You are Jehovah Tsidkenu, the Lord my righteousness, or Jehovah Shalom, the Lord my peace." We can call on Jehovah Rophe, who is "the Lord my healer," or Jehovah Jireh, "the Lord my provider." We thank Him for our peace, our healing, our provision, and our righteousness.

Prayer is all about relationship. Spouses may receive praise for what they do, but they love recognition for who they are. We praise God for who He is. Then we thank Him for the blood to enter the holiest place and begin to magnify God with other tongues. This is the prayer of worship.

"Thy kingdom come" means to establish your day for the kingdom of God. The fruits of the kingdom are righteousness, peace, and joy. I begin to thank Him for right standing, for I am flooded with peace and joy today. Then I extend the boundaries of His kingdom to my family. "Make my kids happy." Also I extend the boundaries of your kingdom to include my pastor and my church.

Now consider "Thy will be done." This is setting our will and priorities to the will of God. We commit to do that which is revealed to us by the power of the Holy Spirit. "If I commit my ways to you and trust you, you will bring it to pass. As I present my body to you, it will be proven what is the good and right way to go."

"As in heaven, so on earth, give us this day our daily bread." This is natural provision as well as physical health. Healing is the children's bread. We confess that Jesus "bare our sicknesses and carried our diseases, by whose stripes we are healed." We pray for the health of our parents, our children, and ourselves. We have soundness of mind. We have strength and power over everything that exalts itself against the knowledge of God. That means freedom from sickness, poverty, fear, worry, and all that Satan or the natural elements send our way.

"Forgive us our sins." This means to check our hearts and motives. Faith does not work when I have unforgiveness in my heart. Reveal to me any person I need to forgive or anyone I am in strife or contention with. You are faithful and just to forgive us our sins when we confess them.

"As we forgive others—" We forgive those who are indebted to us.

"And lead us not into temptation." This is where we gird ourselves up through prayer, submitting ourselves to God and resisting the

Devil. We are not going to fall but fight the good fight of faith. I am not ignorant of the Devil's tactics. I build myself up and resist him.

"Deliver us from evil." This means that we must put our armor on. We must know salvation is sure and be devoted to the Word of truth when faced with natural human facts. As we devote ourselves to the Word, we stand in righteousness, carry the message of peace, stay in an attitude of faith, and quench every fiery dart of Satan.

Then we thank God for His mighty, warring angels that "hearken unto His Word to perform it." We take communion and are in communion every day with Jesus. His atoning blood is our protection for our families, our churches, and our nation.

The prayer of devotion is not intended as a corporate prayer. Many people do not know how or do not want to pray for themselves, so they come to church, and that is the only place they pray. Then they want others to pray about their stuff.

For example, many prayer meetings go on and on because people want others to pray for their kids, their husbands, things that should be part of their personal prayer time. The lack of prayer in this area shows up in church. Paul said in Galatians, "For every one ought to prove their own work" and to bear their own burden (Galatians 6:4, 5) as well as the burden of one another. There is a burden to share, but there are those God expects and holds us accountable to carry to Him.

CHAPTER 16
SPIRITUAL TRANSFERENCE

A lady who ran an apartment block asked me to go to the hospital to pray for her husband. I knew them from the time they spent visiting my father-in-law, and she knew something about God. This man had a bad case of diabetes, and the surgeon was going to remove his leg on Monday.

I went in to see him on the weekend. As I prayed for him, I felt the tangibility of the intangible presence of God on my hands as I lowered them to pray for him. Monday came, and the doctor said he did not have to do surgery because the leg was healing.

Laying on of hands is one way of transferring the anointing. In the transference of spirits, individuals can receive demon spirits as well.

At a bar where an exotic dancer performs her art, a man experiences a shaking phenomenon. Through idolatry, a spirit binds itself to the man's soul. A spirit of lust may open the door to perversion and other maladaptive behavior.

It may enter the body, depending on the depth of the entrenchment.

Soul ties can be broken, but strongholds have greater strength and involve greater strategy, as they involve multiple systems (and demons).

I believe we don't necessarily have to be expert practitioners on deliverance or self-deliverance. The Devil is no match for the Holy

Spirit in us. If we want more power, we want more of Him. If we want more of Him, we must offer Him a holy temple to live in.

Physical Gestures Empowered against the Enemy

Moses held up his arms in the battle against the Philistines. As long as his arms were up, the battle turned in their favor. When he got tired and let down his arms, the enemy prevailed over them. The spiritual significance of this is that physical things can be empowered by God against the Enemy.

A gesture when one is under the anointing may release the Holy Spirit upon people. Laying on of hands has great blessing and is called an "elementary doctrine" in Hebrews 6:2.

Other actions such as anointing with oil, water baptism, or partaking of bread and wine in Holy Communion carry spiritual power. They sometimes precede manifestations, such as physical healing or freedom from demonic attachment.

For example, one lady was bound into the homosexual lifestyle, and she had people lay hands on her for healing prayer. She said, "I am not a lesbian anymore." How is that possible? A parent may have violated the father-daughter trust and relationship. A spirit will always usurp pain or shame and attach itself with a lie over the area of vulnerability. It is said of Jesus that He came to heal all who were oppressed by the Devil. Jesus laid hands on most of the people He ministered to.

Sometimes the reason we are not seeing results is because we do not follow the admonition in Mark 16 to "lay hands on the sick and they shall recover." If this is an elementary doctrine (Hebrews 6), that means we just do it as part of our Christian discipline.

Human reason wants to attach some work to receiving from God. God is not holding back anything. He has given us all things pertaining to life and godliness. They are in His promises. It is up to us to ask and receive as a child from a loving heavenly Father.

Laying on of Hands

The laying on of hands for the transference of spiritual power is what Hebrews 6:2 calls an "elementary doctrine." This is not to be confused with Paul's warning against impulsive laying on of hands for instating a person into office in 1Timothy5:22. Even Jesus made it a part of the Great Commission in Mark16:18.

Some persons have been wary of an unhealthy transference if they are prayed for by demonized persons.

John Wimber[8] talks about people laying hands on one another. "The Holy Spirit is in your life. Trust Him. There's not a perfect person alive on the earth." He talks about fear too. "We need to have more faith in God's ability to bless us than Satan's ability to deceive us."

The ability to bless, whether through music, emotion, or laying on of hands, has been given to us by God. The same instruments God commanded to be employed in worship were used by pagans in idol worship of the images set up by King Nebuchadnezzar. It is not the instrument, but in whose hands it is played.

Some people play instruments, and they sound like a blacksmith working on the anvil. Others have developed and honed their gifts to become sensitive to the anointing of the Holy Spirit. Any gift can be employed for good or bad. Laying on of hands is similar. One is of no consequence. The other has great power to bless.

---

[8] Roberts, Dave, The Toronto Blessing, pg.140 Kingsway Pub., Eastborne, 1994.

On spiritual transference there are many ways that people can be infiltrated by demons. Any recurring sin creates a stronghold for demons. Drugs, music, or illicit sexual intercourse open doors for people to receive demons. Demons can be passed on through the bloodline. How we get free is more important than how we got into bondage, although it may be important to know how they got in.

Anointing with Oil: Lifting up Holy Hands

Other ways of transference are accomplished through the anointing with oil, representing consecration and healing. Oil also symbolizes the joy of the Holy Spirit (Isaiah 61:3; Hebrews 1:9). The vessels of the five foolish virgins had no oil. They had all the trappings of a wedding parade but were not able to enter.

We are His temple, where the glory of His presence dwells. What significantly distinguishes us from religious ideation is that Christ is alive and that He desires to manifest His glory in relationship to us. It is the resurrection that gives us the power. How can He be released if not by the physical action empowered by the Spirit?

Paul said, "I would that men pray everywhere, lifting up holy hands unto God." Why lift up hands? The physical action is both an extolling of one that is greater as well as a submission of self. In the Spirit there is a parallel action that we do not see. This action, though, is seen by the Enemy, and it begins to set up an ambush against him. It is impossible for ministers to impart a blessing to their congregation without raising their hands.

Having begun in the Spirit, shall we continue in the flesh? With some chagrin, Paul states the futility of it. He berated Peter for cajoling with the circumcised Jews in the synagogue.

Prayer and Declaration

We have not asked. For some reason, we feel we are not worthy, or perhaps God is not much interested in our physical well-being. He is interested, and He does want to bless us. The psalms are full of the Lord expressing His mercy and goodness.

Psalm 23 talks about those blessings following us all the days of our lives. His benefits to us are outlined in Psalm 103, where God "crowns us with lovingkindness and tender mercies." He "daily loadeth us with benefits." This psalm finishes with a military reference by using the term "Lord of Hosts." This speaks of the holy angels that in other psalms are said to "do his pleasure." Angels that "excel in strength" and angels that "hearken unto the voice of His Word."

We also must speak the Word more into situations. The situations are temporal, but the Word is eternal. I have mentioned the relationship between facts and truth.

This is why we must speak the Word not as an empty chatter. Paul said he fought "not as one that beats or bats into the air." We should use the Word like a well-honed instrument, a sword that strikes terror through the Enemy's camp.

We ought not to fight like one beating the air. It is essential to know that we have a real enemy and that tongues are great instruments to be used against our Adversary.

Baby Talk

Beating into the air is talk that is something like baby talk. It is not really distinguishable or of any significance. This is why we must have Spirit-empowered prayer. We must pray the Word.

Tongues play a part in entering in to the oracles of God. They create a capacity to receive more revelation.

God must get somewhat tired of hearing our empty chatter. He wants a real conversation. He wants to release deep things into our spirit out of His heart.

Jesus said, "I will pour water on him that is thirsty, and floods upon the dry ground." The well of God is deep, and it is supplied by an underground river of revelation and refreshing. Psalm 42:7 says, "Deep calleth unto deep, and a person of understanding draws it out."

Out of understanding comes wisdom. God uses our level of understanding to lead us with His wisdom. If we have not set our hearts to knowing God in His Word, we cannot receive the wisdom for living.

Partly this is where tongues comes in. When we pray in tongues, we are praying the mysteries of God. We are also magnifying God with our spirits. Angels and demons are watching.

All creation is groaning under the weight of the fall. In our bodies we await redemption. We are not praying sense prayers out of our own minds, but we look to God for illumination into our spirits. We pray for wisdom from the position of God's perspective.

Some of those tongues can be interpreted for wisdom in our daily walk with God, but militant spiritual warfare is directed against the Enemy. It does not require our understanding but our trust. There is a spiritual language for spiritual warfare. We have the Word, but we need the Holy Spirit to pray through us in this manner.

My feeling is that we don't pray in tongues enough, so we never get to the place of getting involved in spiritual warfare. The Lord is waiting for us to set some time aside, to just minister unto Him, but also to lend Him our voices. The Holy Spirit is powerfully going to make intercession for the saints. Some of this is to raid the Enemy's camp and take back what he has stolen.

The Spirit of God raises up a standard against the Enemy. When the Enemy comes in with a flood of generational iniquity, there are bounds that he cannot pass over. We have a part of setting up those bounds by praying in the Spirit. He cannot enter.

Territorial Churches

This is why territorial churches are so important. They are the gatekeepers for the community. Even coming under the covering of a church can still the warfare in one's home.

God's mighty angels are watching over God's Word to perform it. "Bless ye the Lord, all ye His hosts, ye ministers of his that do his pleasure"(Psalm 103:21). These are angelic warriors. They stand guard over God's people and God's treasures. When we make corporate declarations according to the Word, these declarations determine the bounds of the enemy. Angels are the guardians and keepers of that Word. The Devil cannot cross over them.

Being Spiritual in a Physical World

He (God) is in us. To the degree that His power is in us, it must find an avenue for release. Voice and action are what allows us to communicate as humans in a physical world.

The spirit is not separate from the physical but operates in conjunction with the visible realm. The spirit realm is greater in power but is utilized in the natural through the action of faith and a Holy Spirit-empowered voice.

CHAPTER 17

A DEMON'S TONGUE? POSSIBLE EXPLANATIONS

I feel that we are not entering into warfare with demons enough in our private prayers. This is something that comes as a result of praying often in tongues.

Confrontation of this nature does not come to me until I have been in prayer for a while. Then a tongue that is foreign to my regular prayer language will appear. This tongue gets involved with the demon. It is exposing and describing the demon's unclean work. It is an ugly, unclean thing. You can immediately tell the difference.

God allows us to get involved with the demon in order to expose it and loosen its hold. The Holy Spirit of God is taking hold of it together with us to break its power. Incapacitating the demon involves locating it and confronting it.

I have regularly dealt with demons like that in prayer. At first I thought I had a demon. I would confess the blood and the name of Jesus Christ as my Lord. This was unfamiliar territory, but I realized I was getting involved with exposing some dark regions and works of Satan.

The purpose of it became known to me. It wasn't foreign, and it seemed like a natural part of intercessory prayer. People listening would think I was manifesting a demon. So I never got involved with that in public. I feel there is an intercessory work of the Spirit that involves demons. It is a spiritual work by the Spirit.

My Prayer Shop

I often did this "dealing with demons" kind of prayer in the middle of the night. I had a house with my piano shop attached. It was at the other end of the house from the bedrooms. I would go there and close the door, and I was pretty much unheard by the rest of the world.

I commented earlier that a couple of times when I was asleep, I remember hearing piano keys in the top register tinkling at the other end of the house in my piano (prayer) shop. I believe God and His holy angels were waking me up for prayer.

I think the Lord longs for fellowship with us. He waits for us in that certain place just as Jesus had communion with the Father on the Mount of Olives. Some of the prayer in the Spirit is for us. We may be in self-deliverance at times because we are interceding not only for others but for ourselves (Romans 8:26–28).

Jesus made it a pattern for prayer when He said, "Deliver us from evil." The Lord knows what we need and will encounter every day. This is why we pray, "Give us this day our daily bread." We are not to live on yesterday's victories.

The Ball of Fire

In the development of the story I gave in the introduction, my father said later that there was a lot going on during that time. He knew more than I did about spiritual things. I was just a young lad. He said that the next day he went throughout the house and commanded the blood of Jesus over it.

Upon reflection I would not say necessarily that demons were involved in the manifestation. It is possible, but where demons are, angels are much greater in power and number for the believer. However, we may have immobilized them (the angels) through ignorance, unbelief, and sin. There was always a lot of warfare (physical and spiritual) in our house.

The Law of Parsimony

The law of parsimony states that we must try to understand a problem at its most obvious and fundamental level. There might have been a natural explanation for the ball of fire or other mysterious events. I analyze most everything that appears odd first on a natural level, checking for possible explanations.

The spiritual in the life of the Christian is a life of faith, that believes it receives before any physical manifestation appears. This is one reason to pray in tongues. Tongues are a physical manifestation reaching into the spirit realm. When something is prayed through into the spirit realm, it will show up tangibly. We have for too long spiritualized the promises. We must begin to appropriate them to our lives.

Paul prayed that we be preserved—body, soul, and spirit. That means we must appropriate the promises for this life as well as the one to come. Although the Devil operates in the sense realm, we need discernment. Not all manifestations should be credited to the Devil.

All diagnostic processes follow the law of parsimony. If one has a headache, a factor may be eye strain or stress rather than perhaps a tumor. The most obvious explanation should not be ignored. Even though someone may only have a headache, it can be prayed for and healed. Action should take place based on scriptural precedence, although scripture is not against taking an aspirin. Spiritual things are more enduring than physical.

Other mitigating factors, such as family backgrounds, a history of dysfunctional patterns, or mental illness in the family, may give some logical explanations. These should be looked into before assumptions of a spiritual nature are drawn up. A history of the presenting problems may offer other clues that are keys to logical solutions.

Even though we are hesitant to attribute something to the Devil, he may have gained access through an infraction. That might mean there are both a logical and a spiritual conclusion. Most often a spiritual conclusion can be validated when it comes to root causes. The symptom will look for other causes.

Many diseases can be attributed to spiritual and emotional elements. Some examples of spiritual/emotional roots could include fear that is rooted in abandonment, anger that is rooted in shame, and sorrow that is rooted in rejection.

Unforgiveness holds itself to anger. With some types of anger, we are angry at ourselves. We feel we cannot measure up, and we fail to forgive ourselves. Then we are always striving to perform. We set goals that we cannot reach, or we feel someone is holding us back from reaching them. Then our inner frustration and anger turns into depression.

Sorrow is the mental suffering of grief often related to rejection. We cannot receive unconditional love from others when we think we are unworthy of loving ourselves.

Fear may keep individuals from receiving unconditional love, as people fear that love will be taken away from them and that they will be abandoned.

Many times spiritual roots are formed in one's childhood, the age of innocence and directives. The individual has not developed his or her capacity to formulate reasoning. This is why as adults we are in arrested development. We must go back there and reformulate patterns of thinking.

Even though there is a measurable symptomatic explanation in the sense realm, there is usually always a spiritual element. Many times this parallel represents the root.

Facts v. Truth: Diseases Are Caused by Germs

We ought not to deny a fact, but a fact has no bearing on establishing truth. Where one appears to intersect with another, saying they are the same is a dichotomy. It cannot be so in measurable physics. Truth is measured in a different sphere and atmosphere. For instance, when we make the connection between diseases and germs, the spiritual realm is not factored into the equation.

We have removed God through analysis of symptom and observation. Jesus said of the woman with the spirit of infirmity in Luke 13:16, "Ought not this woman being a daughter of Abraham whom Satan hath bound, lo, these eighteen years be loosed from this bond?"

Spiritual roots, such as fear, anger, or sorrow, sometimes show up in physical symptoms. Our whole spirits, souls, and bodies (see 1 Thessalonians 5:23) are interwoven in complexity to make up who we are. That is not to say that some things cannot be measured in a scientific laboratory. Sometimes these are essential in revealing deficiencies, abnormalities, or functioning. Jesus is still the healer, but sometimes He may use science and analysis if it is available to us.

On spiritual issues we want to appear as missionaries for God in foreign lands, yet they know more about the Devil than we do. We have experienced God only on prayers in human action or with emotional support and feeling. Symptom and observable data are the rule for the physical world. We say, "As far as the Devil goes, we know he exists, but he is not much of a distraction to us on a personal level. For the most part our prayers just give us moral support."

This kind of reasoning may be what the Bible refers to when it says that we have a form of godliness, but deny the power thereof. The Word of God is called the sword of the spirit for a reason. True spirituality will necessitate warfare. We can choose a form of godliness that is much easier but makes us no threat to the Enemy. We have given the Word of God no effect through our traditions.

I have a confession in bold letters taped to my desk. It reads, "I claim absolute exemption on the basis of the blood of the Lord Jesus Christ from interference with my mind or imagination. I break all satanic power over my house, the land on which it stands, and my leased properties. I claim my authority as the rightful owner." I can claim the same exemption from attack on my physical body, my loved ones, and my finances (or on my computer)!

We cannot be passive when it comes to spiritual things. There is no spiritual vacuum, no neutral ground. Either we assert our authority, or the Devil will. We must be vigilant against him. First Peter 5:8 says, "Be sober, be vigilant for your adversary—the devil walketh about seeking whom he may devour." Sobriety must be held in all areas of life and addictions.

We tend to medicate ourselves with this lifetime. We ought not to be intoxicated with the flesh, the world, or materialism. We should be addicted to Jesus, our families, His Word, and the fellowship of His saints.

CHAPTER 18
THE HEALING MINISTRY OF JESUS

An Example of Healing

When I was a young teenager, my grandma had a problem with her leg. It had big sores that would not heal. She would spend hours a day in bed with her leg up, applying dressings and roll-up bandages.

There was an apostolic church in Plum Coulee, where they lived. The church taught divine healing and believed in the gifts of the Spirit. I remember Grandma subscribing to the *Voice of Healing* magazine.

Even though Grandpa was a very stoic, old colony Mennonite, Grandma had more sense. She would slip cookies and quarters into my pocket when I would go home from visiting my grandparents.

The minister from this church came down one day to pray for her in her bed. She told me he had said very assuredly, "Now it will get better." And it did. Her leg healed up.

I am not sure if in subsequent years she had more problems, but along with the healing program that Jesus commissions us to in Mark 16:18, there needs to be teaching on faith. There needs to be faith for healing as well as for salvation in the atonement of Christ.

Peter said, "By whose stripes you were healed." Salvation was for body, soul, and spirit. Paul prayed that "you may be preserved, body, soul, and spirit." All are important. Even Jesus did physical healings on the Sabbath, indicating His coming was not only for the spiritual, but He also demonstrated the importance of healing for the physical body. Healing is the children's bread.

Many of the miracles recorded in the Bible involved the people's faith. Jesus required individual faith to move. Even today we cannot disregard our faith. We must give attention to the Word. One reason we are weak in faith is because we are unfamiliar with God's Word.

Faith comes by hearing and making a recitation of it in our hearts. Faith also comes by building ourselves up in prayer. This is why we pray much in tongues (see Jude 20). This releases a river of the supernatural into our lives for whenever we need it.

Understanding the different types of prayer is essential to receiving. Jesus needs us to do our part. Prayer is God's method of our receiving from Him, for what He has to give.

Jesus ministered to the sick the same way we do. He operated in the gifts of the Spirit, which are available through "the every individual part," which the body of Christ supplies. The church together as His body represents the Spirit without measure. That is how Jesus ministered. We must belong to a church that believes and teaches the manifested rewards of faith. Biblical example supports this.

I have given some accounts of healing and each individual's faith step as they were recorded in the gospels. Jesus never refused to heal anyone. He expressed the will of the Father, who is merciful to all. Even the adulterous woman or the demoniac from Gadarene received mercy and deliverance. It is always God's will to show mercy.

The Leper (Mark 1:40–45)

The leper had faith in the will of God. He said with his mouth, "If thou wilt thou canst make me clean." Jesus removed all doubt as to His will for healing by saying, "I will, be thou clean."

The Centurion's Servant (Matthew 8:5–10)

The centurion had experience with commanded authority. He understood the force of words and had an extraordinary revelation of Christ.

The Woman with the Issue of Blood (Mark 5:24–34)

This was a desperate woman. She had heard of Jesus, and somewhere the hope she had lost became faith, for she spoke in her heart, "If I but touch," before she even received.

Jairus's Daughter (Mark 5:21–24)

Jesus put out all the unbelief from the room. Sometimes we shouldn't share everything with everyone. Some people are just sympathy donors. Sympathy only draws attention, but it is compassion that releases healing. Jesus invited in the guardians of the girl, her mother and father. Jesus respects lines of authority. Jesus spoke in faith even though their daughter was dead. He said she was sleeping. He "calls things that be not, as though they were."

Here we recognize that many people die before their times. Jesus represented the express will of God by bringing her back from the dead.

The Nobleman's Son (John 4:46–54)

The nobleman was wiser than his peers. He had a deep revelation of Christ. When tested with the words, "Go thy way, thy son liveth," he went without hesitation.

Peter's Mother-in-Law (Luke 4:38, 39; Matthew 8:14, 15)

This fever was no ordinary fever, but it had a spiritual attachment. It seems that the power of the Devil was being manifested in this affliction. Otherwise, there would not have been an entity to rebuke. You cannot rebuke something that does not have a personality.

Not only did the spirit leave when evicted, but her strength and vitality also returned immediately. She went back to how she was used to, taking care of others in "ministering unto them."

On Faith

Proverbs 30:28 says, "The spider taketh hold with her hands, and therefore is in king's palaces." We need to grab on to some things and hang on with tenacity.

Spiritual things cannot be received on physical terms. The inward man is the real you. The outward man is decaying. As the inward man is being renewed day by day, it finds something to grab on to by what the Bible promises we can have. Many Christians have little stamina in their will.

Healing is the children's bread. It is part of the manifestations in the church. Different prayers may be necessary in some conditions, but we can be sure of His will for us. Jesus never refused one who came to Him for healing.

Some healings involve a command, and others receiving an authoritative word spoken in faith. Jesus rebuked the spirit of infirmity that had held the woman in bondage for eighteen years

Healings may involve the other person's faith. We can make intercession for our loved ones, but we cannot usurp their free will. The individual's lack of faith may stand in the way. We can, however, bind our Adversary, Satan, who may be causing some of the blindness and confusion of their hearts.

CHAPTER 19
TEN KINDS OF PRAYER

Effective spiritual warriors must have some knowledge about prayer. It is first necessary to establish communion with the Father. This is where we developed the discipline of having devotions. Devoting ourselves to God is essential to each new day.

The next step is to gain more results through prayer. Some confusion exists in not understanding the role of prayer in spiritual warfare. Not every prayer is results-oriented. We worship God through prayer. We build ourselves up through prayer. These are inward but nevertheless essential to fulfilling the Lord's commission of going into the world with the gospel.

Several of the rules for prayer contradict one another. One say, "Keep on asking," and another says, "Ask only once and then give thanks." It is essential to understand that each prayer has its own design and purpose.

Praying with all manner of prayer may be contrasted by the following designations within this chapter.

The Prayer with Other Tongues (1 Corinthians 14:18)

This is a prayer by the spirit. This prayer does not involve the understanding but submitting our minds, our will, and our tongues to the river that springs up from our innermost being. It is a spiritual language. Jesus said, "Out of your innermost being shall flow rivers of living water." We must speak (in faith) before we receive the utterance.

The Prayer of Consecration and Dedication (Mark 14:36)

"And He said, Abba Father, all things are possible unto thee, take away this cup from me..." This is dedicating ourselves to God. This could be used where we don't know the will of God and have no idea what God wants, but have also committed ourselves to doing His will or where we do know the will of God but don't want to do it. This is the only kind of prayer that uses an "If it be Thy will."

The problem with using this kind of prayer in other contexts is that it destroys faith. Faith begins where the will of God is known. If we don't know God's will, how can we possibly pray in a confident faith.

The Prayer of Agreement

Jesus said in Matthew 18:19, "If two of you shall agree on earth as touching anything that they shall ask, it shall be done for you by my father which is in heaven." This requires two Christians to pray together. A verse in Deuteronomy 32:30 says, "How should one chase a thousand and two put ten thousand to flight except their Rock had sold them and the Lord had shut them up?" This verse might be applied to the prayer of agreement where ones prayer is increased ten times. Regardless of the formula, the promise is there to increase the results of your prayer. This prayer works if two of you *agree*. If you are not in agreement, the prayer won't work. There is a risk involved. The other individual can mess things up for you.

In Matthew 18:20 Jesus seals the prayer as the guarantor, "For where two or three are gathered together, 'I am there to carry out the agreement."

The Prayer of Fellowship

This is when you spend time with God. More than any prayer, this prayer assures our hearts that we have not been abandoned. There are not many rules for this. We are not coming to ask for anything. We're just coming to spend time with our Father.

First Thessalonians 5:17 may refer to this kind of prayer when Paul says to "pray without ceasing." Here we stay in an attitude of prayer where we share every moment with the Father.

The Prayer of Intercession

Romans 8:26 indicates the Holy Spirit is there to help us to pray when we don't know how to pray. This could be a prayer for ourselves or for others. This could involve various kinds of prayers, but we must do the praying. It can be a combination of prayer with the understanding or in tongues. Sometimes it will involve spiritual warfare. The intensity of the prayer may be determined by the intensity of the problem. This prayer can be initiated by God (who may gives us a burden to pray) or by ourselves.

The Prayer of Faith

Mark 11:24 says, "Therefore I say unto you, What things soever you desire, when you pray, believe that you receive them and you shall have them." This prayer could be prayed for ourselves. In every prayer God has a part to play, and we have a part to play too.

We must first desire. Then we are to believe at the moment of asking. The desires should not be out of line with God's Word. After we pray our desire, we are to believe we have it (before we see it).

We must also remember that when we stand praying (Mark 11:25), we ought to forgive anyone who comes to our minds. This might be a hindrance to receiving from this prayer.

The Prayer of Commitment

1Peter 5:7 says to "cast all your care upon him for he careth for you." We must learn to cast our cares upon the Lord if we want to pray in faith. This prayer creates an atmosphere of peace where God can move. It is more difficult to receive from God in an atmosphere of fear and anxiety.

Philippians 4:6–8 tells us not to worry about anything but to make our requests known to God. Then His peace that passes understanding will keep our hearts and minds in Christ Jesus. We must not be anxious about things but give them to God.

Binding and Loosing

The text on binding and loosing is found in Matthew 18:18. The context of this passage applies to church discipline. What we allow on earth, heaven will allow; what we forbid on earth, heaven will forbid. This might be a clue as to answering some questions, "Why did God allow this to happen?" He permits or allows in our lives what we permit. He has done all he will do by sending Jesus to the cross, it is our move.

We may also apply this prayer to our authority over demon spirits. This is a key to unlocking the kingdom of God.

Matthew 18:19 says, "I give you the keys *of* the kingdom" It does not say that He gives us the keys *to* the kingdom.

We have been given the keys *of* the kingdom. We can lock and unlock anything in the kingdom. God trusts us with the keys. The keys of the kingdom are the promises of God and the authority that is ours in Christ.

The difference between binding and loosing is that in binding the Devil we stop Satan's actions and effectively tie him up from distraction. In loosing the Devil we pry his fingers off and remove him from the situation.

Commanding Power

John 14:12 says, "Verily Verily I say unto you, He that believeth on me, the works that I do shall he do also, and greater..." This is where we rebuke the Devil and demand our rights as a Christian. Commanding power is moving within our authority. It is illustrated in John 14:12–14, where we *demand* something in His (Jesus) name.

Peter commands the man (see Acts 3) "in the Name of the Lord Jesus Christ, get up."

Mark 11:23 says that "whosoever shall *say* unto this mountain, be thou removed and cast into the sea." The verse doesn't illustrate a prayer but rather commanding something to happen. Verse 24 is a prayer, but verse 23 tells us to speak to the mountain (instead of about the mountain, …round and round we go!)

Faith comes by hearing, but faith is released against a problem through words and actions. One may be built up in faith through the hearing of the Word, but it is released against a problem through word and action. We may have the strength from eating and exercise to move a piano, but we must actively mobilize our bodies to the task.

Acts 14:9 tells us an impotent man had the faith to be healed but still sat there crippled. It wasn't until Paul commanded with a loud voice, "Stand upright on your feet," that he leaped up and walked.

Commanding evil spirits might be like times when your dog follows you and you say, "Go on home." The dog doesn't listen until you stop and command it to go home with authority in a loud voice. Then it listens.

We must believe what we say will happen in order to be effective. Our word must be good. Mark 11:23 has two different words for *say*. The first phrase says that you have to believe what you regularly say comes to pass. Then you can believe it when it is time to command a mountain.

The Prayer of Praise, Thanksgiving, and Worship

Hebrews 13:15 says, "By him therefore let us offer the sacrifice of praise to God continually, that is the fruit of our lips giving thanks to his name." We are to offer up spiritual sacrifices as lively stones being built into a spiritual house to be a holy priesthood. (see 1Peter 2:5.) Praise is ministering to the Lord. Praise and worship are the highest kind of prayer. Praise has to do with our words. These are words that commend God for something He is doing, has done, or will do. It is also the giving of thanks.

As New Testament priests, it is our job to offer up sacrifices to God. That is our job description.

Worship is the sum total of all of our actions, attitudes, and being. It is reverence and honor directed at God for who He Is. Worship is not a feeling. Worship involves a cost, the cost of our lives.

CHAPTER 20

DAILY PRAYER: DELIVER US FROM EVIL

The Lord gave us the pattern for prayer in Matthew 6:9.

If We Forget to Pray, We Will Have More Trouble

Prayer is a Christian discipline necessary for living the Christian life. How can we abide in Christ without talking or listening for what He has to say? It may be that some of our trouble comes for a lack of prayer. The Lord's Prayer is a daily prayer. We should pray every day, "Lord, deliver us from evil." James 5:13 says, "If any is afflicted, let him pray."

If We Forget to Pray, We May Be Sinning

First Samuel 12:23 says, "God forbid that I should sin against the Lord in ceasing to pray for you; but I will teach you the good and the right way." *Prayer may involve a higher commitment in life than even earthly relationships, covenants, and commitments.* First

Corinthians 7:5 says, "Defraud ye not one the other except it be with consent for a time, that ye may give yourselves to fasting and prayer."

Intercession: A Special Gift?

Everyone everywhere is commanded to pray, lifting up holy hands to the Lord. This is universal. Although all are called to a prayer and evangelize, not all enter into it to the same degree.

Intercession with diversity of tongues may have a specific manifestation in a particular area. In instances where some are involved in spiritual warfare, they are given a breaker anointing in the use of militant tongues. There is a breaker anointing for a region to strategically bind and loosen territorial strongholds. This is where a few go before into a region in militant intercession to do battle for the kingdom of God. Militant intercession may also involve a period of fasting and setting oneself apart in strategic array.

The corporate intercessor may receive greater utterance and fluency in dealing with ranking spirits and territorial hierarchies as the body of Christ becomes strategically aligned. Authority is preeminent if power is to be imposed. We all have power, but we do not possess all authority. Biblical structure is a key to mobilizing authority. As we are moving in he (Satan's kingdom) must move out.

However, we need to count the cost. It is about staying the course. One cannot be a visiting pastor who is working part-time from another parish. The Enemy knows how to play catch. We are the fools.

This gift is resident in the intercessor, but it is limited because of authority structures.

This is not to say that one has greater power, favor, or access to the kingdom than another. We are to desire earnestly all God has for us. It is God who has anointed us. To whatever degree we walk in that anointing is an individual thing.

Spiritual warfare may include the understanding, but has a dimension where people must trust their inward voice or unction. This is particularly essential when we are moving into militant tongues. They are specific in function and utterance, and sometimes they will include names and commands. This may not always be revealed to our understanding.

I feel we do not honor this calling enough. We all are called to pray, but not everyone seems to move in the Spirit to the same degree. The utterance gifts are specific just like prophecy or teaching.

For example, although one may be used in delivering a word of prophecy, this gift may not be as resident as for the one who stands in the office of the prophet. Although prophecy is one of the utterance gifts, it is a gift of inspiration in intelligible speech (or with the understanding).

The same may be said of the office of the intercessor. All believers have the same access and standing. Satan is forever a defeated foe. The kingdom of God has an open heaven. Jesus passed through the heavens. His death on the cross split the rocks, and rent the veil to the Holy of Holies in the temple. Graves were opened as the earth quaked (trembled), and the dead received resurrected bodies. It is from this position of victory that we shatter strongholds, kingdoms, and dominions on the earth.

Paul says that we ought to desire earnestly the best gifts. When one desires to enter into the Spirit in order to move governments and begin to rule with the kingdom of God, the kingdom of darkness trembles. Its rulers and powers are shaken. They must give up thrones and dominions.

Abraham in relationship and conquest under the old covenant had power with God on earth. All he had to do was place his foot on a piece of ground, and it was his. As far as he could walk, God had promised it to him.

The disciples were astounded at the power of Jesus' commission to the seventy. They said to Jesus, "Lord, even the devils are subject unto us through thy Name. And He said unto them, I beheld Satan, as lightning, fall from heaven." Jesus may have been in prayer, while those seventy were doing the work of the kingdom.

The Spirit of God intercedes through us. He prays through us, initially through tongues and then with Spirit-inspired understanding. When we pray according to 1 Corinthians 12, there is an order. "I will pray/sing with the spirit. I will pray/sing with the understanding."

The order here is significant. Effective prayer is spiritual prayer. Out of the overflow of our spirits, we begin to pray with our understanding.

In intercession we may pray the revealed will of God and then pray with tongues. As we then interpret those tongues, we pray prayers by the inspiration of the Holy Spirit with our understanding. This is where the gifts of revelation come into operation.

Interpretation is not only a corporate gift for the corporate body but also an effective personal prayer language.

Prayer Is Our Way of Receiving God's Gifts as well as His Goodness

Praying in tongues is paramount in releasing the gifts of revelation, such as the word of wisdom, the word of knowledge, and the discerning of spirits. These occupy a significant part in praying effectively.

Although God does make use of our great minds and understanding, it is only as we are illuminated by the Holy Spirit and the Word that we are effective. Wisdom comes from a heart of understanding. The reason we may lack insight in certain areas of our lives might be because we fail to seek first the Lord's will and kingdom and receive the desires He has placed in our hearts. Sometimes we lack because we simply don't ask (see James 4:2).

Sometimes we need to set ourselves apart for a time to get some answers from God. Daniel set his face unto the Lord, to seek by prayer and supplication with fasting, in sackcloth and ashes. He prayed in Daniel 9:19, "O Lord, hear O Lord, forgive; O Lord, hearken and defer not." (O Lord, hear and act). James also said, "The earnest prayer of a righteous man availeth much." Jesus said, "Ask and it shall be given you, seek and ye shall find, knock and the door shall be opened unto you" (Matthew 7:7).

The apostles regarded prayer as the most important employment that could engage their time and attention. Acts 6:4 says, "But we will give ourselves continually to prayer, and to the ministry of the Word."

CHAPTER 21
VARIOUS FORMS OF PRAYER

Crying unto the Lord

The people "cried unto the Lord" in Joshua 7:6–9 and Judges 6. This is something I have experienced when my spirit is entirely overwhelmed. It is not inspired by the Spirit (like a roar that has intent and power). Crying to the Lord is the human element as if someone were in distress. It is an overwhelming feeling of hopelessness, as if somewhere in a deep well.

The psalmist wrote in Psalms142:3 "When my spirit was overwhelmed within me…" This sometimes represents a long period of deep pain or a feeling of being *lost*. It is not distinctive, but it is the voice of the soul.

Psalm 55:2 says, "Attend unto me and hear me; I mourn in my complaint and *make a noise*." Some things are too deep for words. I have found sometimes after a night of these kinds of agonizing noises that God has heard my despair and changed something for me.

Dialogue

Different forms of prayer were offered in the Bible. Abraham took the form of *dialogue*. God and man draw near and talk to each other in Genesis 18 and 19. This developed into intercession for the righteous for wicked Sodom. Jesus talked to His Father in John 17. Jesus received prophetic insight through His prayer. He even prayed for us in verse 20.

Personal Prayer

In Mark 11:24, Jesus says, "Whatsoever you desire, when you pray." We are to desire, and we are to believe we receive when we pray. Abraham talked to God about personal things. He says in Genesis 15:2, "Lord God, what wilt thou give me, seeing I go childless." Hannah poured out her heart to God for a child, and God granted her request.

Corporate Prayer

Corporate prayer was made in Acts 4:29–31, "Consider their threats while you stretch forth your hands to heal in the Name of your holy child Jesus… when they had prayed, the place was shaken… and they spoke the Word with boldness." The Lord appeared unto Solomon, saying, "If my people which are called by my Name shall humble themselves and pray, seek my face and turn from their wicked ways, then will I hear from heaven, forgive their sins and heal their land" (1 Chronicles 7:14).

Pouring out Your Heart

David pours out his heart to God in Psalms 42:4 where he says, "When I remember these things, I pour out my soul in me; for I had gone down with the multitude..." This may be more reflective of the extreme emotions or moods he encountered. It does not hold the same desperation as crying to the Lord. He does not go to God with fixed and orderly petitions so much as to simply pour out his feelings and desires to God. Whether he is depressed, troubled, joyful, or serene, his moods are a reflection of his heart.

David is not afraid to complain to God about his situation. Although he begins with pouring out his heart and feelings, he often ends with a word from God about his situation.

Elements like praise, adoration, and thanksgiving may be a part of communing with the Lord. We must also incorporate a time for reflection. Prayer is a place for receiving vision, an observatory where problems are solved and creative ideas are spawned. Prayer is a place of vision, rest, and rejuvenation.

Prayer Posture

What are we to do with our bodies while we are praying? I used to walk and pray a lot in tongues in my shop. I have some favorite places where I can be alone. I have a waterfall that I walk to that is about a twenty-minute hike from my house. I jump the rocks and sit in the middle of the rushing stream. That is one place I go sometimes when I feel like I need to be vocal (I also listen there.)

We are exhorted to pray without ceasing. That is pretty much anywhere. Jesus stood and prayed, lifting up His eyes to heaven.

In the garden Jesus was withdrawn from His disciples about a stone's cast where He kneeled down and prayed. He fell on His face and prayed in Matthew 26:39.

The soul may be crying or reaching out to God in earnest prayer, but we need to be directed and specific. We can do this no matter what the employment of our bodies.

Times and Places of Prayer

David said, "Seven times a day will I praise thee." This could be a form of prayer. Daniel kneeled at his window and prayed three times a day. Peter and John had a routine where they went up to the temple in the morning at the ninth hour to pray. Peter prayed on the rooftop!

Jesus spent the night in prayer before He chose His twelve disciples (see Luke 6). Jesus needed to pray after great successes too. He would often spend the whole night in prayer in the Mount of Olives. Many times He arose "a great while before day." "He went out and departed into a solitary place and there prayed."

He would pray when there was special trouble or perhaps when it was mealtime. Peter and John prayed before the unsaved in prison. Paul says we ought to pray everywhere, lifting up holy hands without wrath and doubting (1 Timothy 2:8).

CHAPTER 22
HELP IN PREVAILING PRAYER

Fasting

Jesus said, "When you fast," indicating that fasting was not an option. Fasting then is a part of our stewardship to God. It is an essential requirement.

A well-known lady who was also a world-class Bible teacher used to fast every Monday. I did that for a while, even though I found myself under a lot of oppression that day. Then I would just fast till supper. Still, we need to put ourselves onto some kind of program. Otherwise it will not happen. The disciples fasted when they chose elders. It was also through fasting that the Holy Spirit commissioned Barnabas and Saul into ministry.

Fasting should always be accompanied by prayer. Otherwise we are just denying ourselves food for a season. Although cleansing our bodies may be an essential physical ritual, in order to have spiritual significance, we must starve off our flesh to feed our spirits.

Heartfelt Earnestness

Earnestness has a lot to do with whether prayer is effective. Keeping a pure heart free from idolatry is essential.

James 5:17 says, "The fervent, effectual prayer of a righteous man availeth much." Sometimes it is the simplicity of a prayer that gains results.

Being resolute and not being of a double mind is essential. James 1:8 says, "He that is of a double mind should not think that he will receive anything from the Lord." David was definite when he said in Psalm 27:4, "One thing have I desired of the Lord, that will I seek after."

It may be necessary to persevere just as the impertinent widow did in imploring the unjust judge.

Keeping a Journal

Keeping a journal of our requests as well as the answers, I have found, is a great help in keeping track (as well as keeping one on track)!

CHAPTER 23

A TREASURE WITHOUT A MEASURE

We have this treasure in earthen vessels that the excellency of the power may be of God and not of ourselves.

Jesus has the Spirit without measure. He is pouring, but we have not the capacity to receive. He desires to give us more.

Inviting Christ into our lives was the greatest treasure we could ever find. We are new creatures in Christ. There is nothing that compares with the joy and newfound freedom in being released from bondage and sin.

Anyone who is in Christ is a new creature. Old things have passed away. All things have become new. Romans 8:11 says that same Spirit (that raised Christ from the dead) comes to dwell in us, and we become His temple. The Lord wants to do more in our lives than what we can ask or think. This is why we need more.

Wine Tasting or Just a Sip Will Do

The Holy Spirit is likened unto wine. The early disciples upon receiving the outpouring in the upper room were staggering around like drunken men. Peter asked, what do you think; it is not even 9:00 in the morning, "these men are not drunken as you suppose…" The spectacle had aroused a lot of people to come check out what they thought was an early morning phenomenon of drunken Jews. Society was aghast at the impropriety; it was yet before 9:00 in the morning where any respecting Jew would pour a glass of wine.

The Holy Spirit had been poured out, and the day of Pentecost had fully come! Have we taken what was begun in the Spirit and tried to perfect it in the flesh?

For Us and/or Others

The first fill-up is the infilling of the Holy Spirit upon our rebirth. This is for regeneration. The second outpouring upon us is for others. Acts 1:8 says, "When the Holy Spirit comes upon you, you shall be my witnesses." I could use more of that power.

It is by one Spirit that we are baptized into the body of Christ. First Corinthians 12:12–13 says, "For as the body is one, and hath many members, and all the members of that one body, being many, are one body: so also is Christ. For by one Spirit are we all baptized into one body, whether we be Jews or Gentiles, whether we be bond or free; and have all been made to drink into one Spirit."

We are members one of another. We have an adversary, and he wants to divide and conquer. He deceives people into taking offense with one another. Why is it so hard for people to get along? We need to come under the influence of the wine of the Holy Spirit! We need the oil of joy to run over us. We need the fountain of living waters to refresh us and make us new!

Oil and Wine

We used to sing, "Give me oil in my Ford. Keep me puttin' for my Lord. Give me oil in my lamp, I pray—" That was a fun song, but the reality is we need the oil of joy for our everyday lives. Joy comes in the morning. Without it, life becomes mundane, and work becomes a toil.

Oil represents the new birth. When the foolish virgins had no oil, they could not enter into the wedding feast. Wine represents the overflow of the Holy Spirit. Water represents the fountain of life, refreshing and cleansing in the Word.

A liter of gas will get my truck started, but if I am making a trip to Alberta from Manitoba, I gas up right to the top, where the needle on the gas gauge is past full. Then I gas up again.

For a major work we need to have a major fill and not expect to make it on a trickle. We must stop periodically for a fill-up. Although the fill-up may begin with a sensational experience and overflow, we must keep ourselves full so that we can always move out of the overflow.

There is full, which still represents the infilling, but then we need an immersion, where we become saturated with the Holy Spirit. We will not have to work up courage or present some witty interjection. God is on us, and He will show up.

This is necessary for the spreading out of the gospel. Otherwise, we invite car salesmen into church to give us the latest formulas and strategies on selling. We see how to work a crowd or person, how we can manipulate conversations, how we can be like Slick Willie in every situation.

When the supernatural begins to show in our churches, we won't have to spend as much advertising with clever motivational slogans. People will just come. They are hungering after God. They are crying inside, "Please show me a God that is real."

Jude 20 gives us one element essential to keeping our spirit tank full. It says, "But ye beloved, building up yourselves on your most holy faith, praying in the Holy Ghost." As we pray in tongues, a river is loosed inside of us, where "out of your belly shall flow rivers of living water."

The difference between a well and a river is *power*. Jesus said that out of a man's heart come forth both bitter and sweet. This indicates the well that he draws from must be kept and protected from being defiled. When our well is fed by the stream of living water, we can create a river.

A Real Gusher!

I had the opportunity of investing in a well drilling company at one time with some of my relatives. These guys were hard workers, but one time they were a little overzealous. The driller (my brother-in-law) had not read his geophysical map of the area. There were underground streams running, and these were under pressure, creating artesian wells.

My brother-in-law sunk down a four-inch hole. It was not sixty feet, and he had a gusher coming up at him in full bore. That was overflowing. In fact, that was an impending disaster. The whole country might have been flooded!

He called in the experts. It took some time. A backhoe had to come in and dig a trench to the ditch. Then another team came in with a huge supply of cement bags and equipment. We eventually got that thing plugged up, and under control, but not without a whole lot of sweat and labor.

That was overflow with an impending flood. I like to think that is how God will work. We have likened God to the refreshing. It is time for a flood, a mighty river of His spirit and anointing for our world.

Water is also a source of power. A hydro dam is not built next to a well but to a river. A well may supply a family or neighborhood, but a power dam can produce enough power to light up a whole city!

Wine, Worship, and Soaking in His Presence

In Calgary, they periodically have *Twenty-Seven-Hour Burns* where there is a continual atmosphere of praise and worship. A new band comes on every two hours. This is a marvelous way to experience God and just set aside time to seek Him. I enjoy the time there just to pray in the Spirit for several hours and bring a lot of things to God.

For the last event I came to there, I arrived at 8:00 p.m. and left at 2:30 a.m. There was just no pressure. I really felt a lifting up and release of oppression as I pushed into God. My voice got strong and clear by the end of my time there, and I knew I had touched God.

The Hebrews have alotted seven terms for worship—*barak*, meaning to kneel before the Lord in reverence and honor; *yodah* and *towdah*, meaning to extend hands in praise; *zamar*, meaning to play instruments and sing; *shabach*, meaning to shout unto God with the voice of triumph while clapping; *halal*, meaning to rave, to boast about the Lord, to be wild until clamorously foolish, or to dance; and *tehillah*, meaning to praise until God's presence is manifested. This is the highest form of praise.[9]

---

[9] *Old Testament Hebrew Lexicon, King James Version*

God inhabits the praises of his people (see Psalm 22:3). When we align our flesh with our spirits, placing demands on it by kneeling, lifting our hands, singing, shouting, clapping, standing, and rejoicing, we give God the highest (techillah) form of praise. This is one way we can find the manifest presence of God.

Let your praise be continually on your mouth. We had a pastor that would always say, "Praise You, Jesus. Thank You, Father. Bless You, Jesus." His heart had a continual overflow of praise to God.

Isn't that what Jesus said? "For out of the heart man brings forth both good and evil." Keeping our hearts with all diligence means to set a watch over our tongues. Giving thanks to God, which is the fruit of our lips, means to rejoice always, "Let them say continually, Let the Lord be magnified, which hath pleasure in the prosperity of His servants" (Psalm 35:37).

This pastor said, "Be in an attitude of expectancy." Expect something from God every day. That might mean just waiting, sometimes in the busyness of life, abiding in that place of rest in Christ. It is in the overflow of His goodness and mercy that He becomes the glory and lifter of our heads. It is that glory that overflows and becomes our rear guard.

CHAPTER 24

SPECIAL MIRACLES, PROPHETIC DREAMS, AND LEVELS OF ANOINTING

Evangelists talk about special miracles, such as gold fillings in teeth, physical lengthening of limbs, or replacement of body parts and organs. Manifestations such as glory clouds and aromas are said to accompany the tangible presence of God. Bethel Church in Redding California regularly has gold glitter, and glory clouds manifesting (you tube.com). One church in Puerto Rico is said to have had the angel of gemstones leaving behind precious stones. Oil would drip from a Bible.

I do not discount the tangibility of God just because I do not necessarily understand it. That God is unusual goes without saying. We just need to look at any species of His created variety and genius. They do have bounds however, natural laws of creation, limitations governed by space and time.

Even though Jesus was the Son of God, He was fully a man and lived in the natural. It was the Holy Spirit that lifted Him into the supernatural. He exercised the gifts of the Spirit the same way we do. An instance occurred at the gate of the city of Nain (see Luke

7). A young man had died, and his funeral procession was so sad it caught Jesus's attention. The man had died before his time. He was an only son of his mother, who was a widow. Jesus never contravenes the will of His Father. He touched the bier and said to the young man, "Arise." The man sat up from the coffin. Jesus gave the man back to his mother.

My experiences in this area may be limited to a couple incidents that I can remember. I was in an intercessory prayer group that would meet every Saturday night. In one prayer setting after Holy Communion, which we would always take before we prayed, there was a fairly dramatic spiritual encounter. After a time of strong spiritual engagement and militant warfare (in other tongues), there was silence for a space of time. A weight of glory filled the room. I did not see anything. I was almost afraid to open my eyes. I could only respond because my mouth was open in awe and wonder. In total silence no one dared to move. It was spiritual, yet it seemed to possess weight.

One time we had a Lutheran minister come to our church. He might have been charismatic because he operated in a gift of healing for the body. There were no other indications. He was a very boring preacher but had this special gift for healing backs. When he laid his hand on you, you would begin to slowly move and stretch out into the most amazing caricatures. People with back problems were said to have had improvements and healing.

One evangelistic meeting I attended had a fairly believable fellow who had played in professional sports most of his life. He professed that he had many reports of people having their teeth filled with gold during his meetings.

Whether or not we see them, there are miracles and special gifts of healing. God has them in heaven, and He is waiting for us to receive them on earth. They are a part of His body ministry because He knows we need them.

Skeptics may ask, "Why would God do such miracles like gold fillings?" This can only be answered in the heavenly paradigm of relationships, *He is our Abba Father!*

Prophetic Dreams

I think our dreams are a part of our cognition and fears. However, there are some dreams that have greater significance, an almost prophetic foretelling.

Just recently I had a dream where I was soaring through the heavens on a zip line, hanging on for dear life. I was flying over the tops of the mountains. It was both exhilarating and scary. Then I went over the top of the most beautiful valley. It was exquisite and full of color. I felt the dream held some relevance to where my life was at—a foretelling.

I had another dream of this large house that was free—a free house! But it was quite removed from regular cities or civilized life, situated in a somewhat abandoned town. Only the local townsfolk lived there.

Well, apparently the Pentecostal church had gotten it and claimed it. But no one individual really owned it or occupied it. People would just go there be-times, from the church, to stay.

Then it turned out that there were creeps in it. It had spooks. I gathered that was because there were no real owners, no one who really had power of attorney over the house.

Some dreams might be related to the amount of antihistamines one might take before bed, but sometimes there are real applications or prophetic revelations. I believe God uses them at times to warn us.

Personal Level of Anointing

Every believer has a measure of rule. We must remain within it in order to receive the anointing that God has given to us for our ministry. We all carry an anointing to minister within our sphere of influence, but every born again believer carries a measure of the anointing. The Holy Spirit is in us when we receive Jesus into our hearts.

Anointed Ministry Gifts

Paul said that more grace was given unto him according to the measure of the gift of Christ. He had the responsibility as an apostle to all the churches, which required more anointing than those ministering on a local level.

God gives us a measure of anointing for our calling. It is our responsibility to be diligent in the effectual working in the measure of every part of the body. According to our responsibilities and spiritual gifts, we will have a greater or lesser measure of the anointing to fulfill those tasks.

The Corporate Anointing

The whole body of Christ is increased when individual believers find and are allowed to use their spiritual gifts. Jesus was anointed of the Holy Spirit without measure. The church is His body. We are to come to the "measure and stature of the fullness of Christ" (Ephesians 4:13,16). This means we are to give more honor to the fivefold ministry perfecting the saints. We need them for our maturity as individuals. Then the Holy Spirit is allowed to "fitly join us together by that which every joint supplieth."

As we give attention and commitment to the body to be compacted together in love, we will achieve the measure of Christ's anointing. Even though there are differences, we strive to stay in the unity of the faith with "the bond of peace" (Ephesians 4:3). We realize that we do not have to totally agree with everything in order to be a vital organism. The wine of the Holy Spirit will help us to stay in joy, even though there are menial tasks to do. Every part of the body is significant and a part of the whole.

This corporate anointing is the greater anointing that Jesus referred to when He said, "Greater things than these shall you do." It is the anointing without limitation. Healings and miracles occur in greater measure through the organized gathering of believers.

The church must have structure and framework involving the fivefold ministry before Christ can begin to fill it. This is why leadership gifts are so important. These bring direction, revelation, and declaration to the body. Leaders may instill hope and confidence to those just starting out in the supportive ministry. The supportive gifts are fundamental in establishing and supporting the leadership structure. No one is insignificant.

CHAPTER 25
SPECIAL TACTICAL SQUAD

Diversity of Tongues in Dealing with the Devil

I believe there is an added dimension in this area of utterance gifts. Diversity of tongues involves various workings, but there is a specific area of dealing with the Devil. This may involve the gift of discerning spirits, but it also involves diversity of tongues, specifically in dealing with demonic strongholds.

Revelation talks about fallen angels that are reserved in chains of darkness for the last judgment. These are not our problem, but there are disembodied spirits on the earth. These free radicals, which for one reason or another were left here under the rule of Satan, have a lease on earth and are here out of some alliances they have made with people and the Devil.

These evil spirits seek to enter human bodies. Some of the ways they gain access are through idols. They come in through the desire of the flesh, the allurement of the eyes, and the quest for worldly power and acclaim.

Jesus conquered these same temptations in the wilderness of testing. How is it that we are still dealing with the same elements of temptation? It is because we are striving against the temptation rather than receiving by faith the victory already accomplished.

Paul said we were no longer debtors to the flesh to obey its dictates because we have the resurrected Spirit of Christ indwelling us (see Romans 8:11).

Our bodies are not yet redeemed. We must present them unto God, a holy sacrifice and offering unto Him. This we cannot do by ourselves. We must pray hard until the resurrected Christ imparts His power into our fragmented, mortal bodies.

This means to pray in the Spirit (tongues) as well as the understanding. Paul prayed more than everybody. If he was in our world (in Calgary) while walking along the LRT tracks, waiting for the train, he might be praying in tongues for that reservoir of faith to be filled.

This is a spiritual work. An ascetic lifestyle (to enter into a disciplined life of restraint) is not enough. We must have a reservoir of the Holy Spirit. Paul said that we need to "walk in the Spirit." Then we will not allow the Devil a foothold.

Although we can stop the activity and strategy of the Devil through binding, we must free his captives. This may require some unfurling of plots and schemes.

We are exhorted to keep ourselves holy so that we can remain separate from becoming enmeshed and entangled in the affairs of this life. This is because part of that entanglement with the world is playing into the schemes of Satan.

Diabolos-Evil Schemer

Devil is derived from the greek diabolis meaning false accuser, slanderer *(1228 diabolos, Strong's Concordance)*. Unfurling plots and evil schemes are part of the reason we need the Holy Spirit to help us to pray with "inarticulate speech" (Romans 8:26). God is giving us a code language to expose and undo the strategies and tactics being employed against us. As we pray in tongues, the Devil's schemes are being exposed.

Huddles and Game Play

An instance of turning the game around on Satan occurred one time when I was in an intercessory prayer group. We would meet every Saturday night for communion and intercessory prayer.

One time as we were praying in other tongues, we began to pray like we were having a conversation with one another. It was like a football huddle where we were strategizing in another language. Jesus had given us the power to do that through the gifts of utterance. I am sure it drove the Devil crazy.

Is it possible to have a conversation human spirit to human spirit in tongues? From a natural perspective this is craziness. How is it that we need to have our mental faculties salved?

Row, Row, Row Your Boat!

When the disciples were having a rough time rowing across the Sea of Galilee in the middle of the night, there was Jesus walking on the water in the distance. The narrative says He would have walked right by them, but they cried out as though they were seeing a ghost. So He changed His direction, came toward them, and jumped over into their boat. This is why we need to call out for and desire earnestly the best gifts. They will not just come to us. We need to yearn for more of God.

They were amazed at Him because they still had not recognized Him or perceived yesterday's miracle of the feeding of the five thousand.

How much does it take to recognize Jesus in our boat? He is supernaturally providing for us, or He is bringing to us a reason to believe in the midst of the irrational.

We always want to reason things out. God sometimes has to bypass our minds in order to effect his intercessory work through our spirits.

This is where a well-practiced and finely tuned dimension of the Spirit comes into play. As we are more accustomed to the voice of the Lord, we can fit into strategizing His way.

CHAPTER 26

FREE WILL: MAN V. GOD... AND THE DEVIL

Joe Average from the, "We've got the power" Church is wondering how to witness to his neighbor and win him over to the Lord. As he considers it, he waits for him in his driveway and talks to him after work.

His neighbor is terse with him and rebuffs him, "Don't give me that Jesus stuff."

In frustration he prays for God to do something. God thinks about it and then sends the Devil to put him into a hammerlock. God says, "Now you will accept Me."

The man still resists, so God sends the Devil again, and the Devil puts him into a headlock and squeezes harder. The man begins to protest, but his will is set against God still. So God says, "Give him the figure-four leg lock!'.

So the man says in submission, "I give up. I give up."

Then God says, "Let him go."

God then takes him by the hand, and they walk away together. God looks him in the eye and says, "Aren't we having sweet fellowship?"

This is the mentality most Christians have of the Devil—that somehow the Devil is God's right hand man in accomplishing His will. We need to see the deceptive schemes of Satan. He loves it when we give God the credit for what he is doing.

We must realize that the Devil is against God. His attacks are designed to kill you and take you out of commission. When he comes in to steal, kill, and destroy, his devices or missiles (fiery darts) are not God's way of perfecting us. God *does not send cancer to test you. It is designed to kill you!*

When the attacks of Satan come, there must be a confrontation. We must deal with the Devil with God's mandate. Jesus came to destroy the works of the Devil. He needs our voice, a voice so empowered by the Holy Spirit that the demons tremble when it speaks.

When God effects change, it is His Word that sits as a refiner's fire and fuller's soap. The Word becomes a hammer that breaks through unbelief.

Jesus said, "Now you are clean through the words I have spoken unto you." The gifts must be recognized in the body in order for Jesus to speak effectively. The offices of administration are there to bring us to completion in Christ. God does not anoint the Devil to that end.

It is the administrations of the body, those called to leadership in the fivefold ministry, that are there "for the perfecting of the saints, for the work of the ministry" (Ephesians 4:11). We need anointed ministers in the Word.

Teachers must be not only skilled but anointed in bringing the Word like a sharp sword that can pierce through ignorance and tradition. Prophets must not only be anointed to bring comfort, edification, and exhortation but also to bring the confrontation of sin and error.

God's Word Is Supernatural

God's Word is supernatural because He is watching over it and performing it. The angels of God have been waiting on us to be employed on earth. By putting God's Word into our heart and speaking it, we send them commands.

We are the ministers of His covenant on the earth. We are the anointed ones. We carry out the will of God on the earth. God must have a voice in the earth.

Psalm 103:20 says, "Bless the Lord ye His angels that exel in strength, that do his commandments." Hebrews 1:14 says, "Are they not all ministering spirits, sent forth to minister for them who shall be heirs of salvation?" We are the heirs of salvation. Psalm 104:4 describes these holy messengers as spirits and ministers of flaming fire, that hearken unto the voice of His Word. Psalm 103:20 says, "Bless the Lord ye his angels that excel in strength, that do his commandments, hearkening unto the voice of his word."

Are not the angels big enough to handle anything the Devil has to offer? They surely are. Then why are they not working?

This is where human reasoning sets in. We think that all the evil that comes to us must have been God's plan. I have news. *The Devil is not on God's payroll.* He has his own agenda. God doesn't need him to conform us to His image. 2 Corinthians 3:18 says, "But we with open face beholding as in a glass the glory of the Lord, are changed into the same image from glory to glory even as by the Spirit of the Lord." It is in beholding Christ that we are changed.

Some things we do just out of ignorance, selfishness, or pride. The Devil uses those things in disrupting the destiny of God for our lives. God doesn't need the Devil to refine us. Persecution always comes for the Word's sake. It is the Word he is after. God sends His Word in Psalm 107:20 and delivers them from their destruction.

The refining comes by the fire of the Holy Spirit. Malachi 3:2 says of God's messenger, "He shall sit as a refiner's fire and as fullers soap." John the Baptist made reference in Matthew 3:11–12 to Jesus sending us His Holy Spirit when he said, "He shall baptize you with the Holy Ghost and with fire… He will thoroughly purge his floor… and burn up the chaff with unquenchable fire."

This testing of motives is what the Word refers to in Ephesians 6, where "the Word of God is sharper than any two-edged sword, piercing even to the dividing asunder of soul and spirit… and is a discerner of the thoughts and intents of the heart."

Jeremiah 23:29 says, "Is not my word like a fire? Saith the Lord; and like a hammer that breaketh the rock in pieces." Do we feel the need for change? Try the Word. It is all that will change us.

Putting a Demand on God's Word

Isaiah 45:11b says, "Ask me of things to come concerning my sons, and *concerning the work of my hands command ye me*." Psalm 138:2b says, "For thou hast magnified thy Word above all thy Name." God honors His Word when we speak it. Because He could swear by one no greater than Himself, He swore by Himself that He would fulfill His covenant to Jacob.

God is a covenant God. He loves covenants because He never changes. His love remains forever. In our world, we have trouble promising to love and cherish our wives, husbands, and families even just for a lifetime.

But God has promised never to leave you or forsake you. He will always love you. He loves to give His Holy Spirit to you. He has made every provision for your lifetime through His precious promises. Second Peter 1:2 says, "By these great and precious promises, He has given us all things pertaining to life and godliness… and has made us partakers of the divine nature."

We need to put a demand on those promises and not allow the Devil's lies and deceptive schemes of unbelief to stop us. God has prepared a table before us. He is preparing a house for us. He is preparing a city for us. Even in this lifetime, God has already made provision for us. Before we even go to the city, if God is leading us there, He has already been there to make preparations.

God likes it when His kids take Him up on His Word. Our house is empty until we realize that "being thoroughly furnished" (2 Timothy 3:17) is for the purpose of good works to others. We must learn to live for others, to give from our hearts.

How can we abound unto every good work if we don't have anything to give? Is God really able to make all grace abound toward us so that we *always have all sufficiency* in all things and may abound unto every good work? We need to have a house that is thoroughly furnished. That may mean an abundant supply of healing and deliverance and an abundant supply of wealth from the table of the Lord.

Psalm 23 says, "Thou preparest a table before me, in the presence of mine enemies." It is not always in favorable conditions that God shows up. He is in the valleys of despair. The book of Psalms reminds us that when we thought nobody cared, there He was to meet all our needs and give us an overflow for others.

We should never discount the day of small things. We may not see a fugitive wilderness experience as David had of any consequence. It was there that David honed his skills and those with him in the wilderness. It was there that they would learn about covenant relationships. They were rejected and displaced lacking even the basic essentials of life; however, God provided and used those days in preparation for ruling in a kingdom.

CHAPTER 27
PRAYING MYSTERIES

The Mysteries of God

Paul said, "He that prayeth in an unknown tongue speaketh not unto men, but unto God; howbeit in the spirit he speaketh mysteries."

The mystery of God has to do with the greatness of our salvation and God's unsearchable wisdom. Even angels do not understand it and are watching in awe. We have an awesome place in the kingdom of God. We are the only ones who have been redeemed.

Paul talked about this awesome calling of God when he prayed for the saints in Ephesus "that they might know the hope of their calling, and the riches of the inheritance in the saints in Christ."

Jesus is not ashamed to call us His brethren. He is the first begotten from the dead. That is a mystery, how that he is the firstborn of many brethren, that we can be born into the same family anas sons of adoption we get to call His Father our Father. That is a mystery. I don't understand that.

Joseph Schellenberg, D.C.C.

Great Is the Mystery of Godliness

It is a mystery how we who have fallen so greatly have a chance at being restored to the kingdom of God.

In the earth, we who are in Christ are set high above principality and power, might, and dominion. This conquest is part of that mystery. Angels desire to look into it. They do not understand.

Through our praying in tongues, God is revealing and exposing the militant strategies of the Devil. We are praying into the realm of the spirit and defeating spirits that operate in the present darkness of this evil world. The Holy Spirit is exposing them, and He is using our tongues to do it.

Paul says that the weapons of our warfare are not carnal but mighty through God to the pulling down of strongholds. These are enemy ramparts, with strategic implementation of bastions and bulwarks behind which operations are conducted within our borders. Prophetic preaching and militant intercession will rout them out.

Our expectation is in relation to our revelation of Christ. Jesus already dealt with the Devil when He died on the cross. Jesus conquered the flesh, the world, and everything that hell, death, and the grave could offer. It is a mystery how we are to defeat the Devil through His name.

The resurrection is the greatest feat and victory of our faith. We have confidence and access to the Father through the high priestly atonement of the blood of Christ. We have boldness and access to the Father's throne. That is a mystery.

CHAPTER 28
DEAL WITH THE DEVIL

Autopilot?

The problem is that God hasn't put us on autopilot in this lifetime. We think we can cruise through life without any warfare.

The Devil strategically still holds regions, landmarks, and sand castles. We must go in and kick the sand in his face. These are mirages and latent thrones of power. He is unseated. Jesus spoiled principality and powers, making a show of them openly, triumphing over them. Then we come along, and he is still sitting there. We need to command him to get off and get out. We are coming in the name of the Lord.

The Lord of Hosts in Psalm 24:7–10 is a military reference denoting strength or the Lord strength in battle. He has already won the battle, but it is up to us to enforce that victory. We must defeat the Enemy with the sword of the Spirit, which is the Word of God. When we do, then the king of glory shall come in. We clear the heavens through militant prayer, confrontation, and proclamation. Jeremiah gave the order to "root out, to build, and to plant." That involves strategy and structure.

The Holy Spirit is empowering us to build. "Except the Lord build the house, the builders build in vain; Except the Lord keep the city the watchman waketh but in vain." We need to have the mind of the Spirit. We need to know the Word like no generation before us. This is the church's finest hour, the hour of entering in to the kingdom of God.

When we deal with the Devil (as Paul did when he commanded them in Christ's stead to be reconciled to God), we will see miracles, healing, and salvation to a much greater degree. The same amount and quality of ministry will bear much greater results. Pastors will think it was their great sermons, and worship leaders will think it was their great talent. Nothing happens in the Spirit until we deal with the Devil.

Anointing Released through Gaze and Command

Paul illustrates an authority on how to deal with the Devil in Acts 13. Here Elymas, the sorcerer, withstands Barnabas and Saul in an attempt to turn the deputy away from the faith. Saul, who was filled with the Holy Ghost, sets his eyes on him and says, "O full of all subtilty and all mischief, thou child of the devil, thou enemy of all righteousness, wilt thou not cease to pervert the right ways of the Lord? And now, behold, the hand of the Lord is upon thee, and thou shalt be blind, not seeing the sun for a season."

Here we see that the anointing of the Holy Ghost can be released through the eyes. The eyes are said to be the windows of the soul. Not all eye contact is spiritual, but in this instance there was a definite transference.

Then we see that strong words are necessary to locate the Devil. He called him a child of the Devil and then revealed his characteristics.

We recognize through this passage that God has given authority to intercept the work of Satan through gaze and command. When the Devil comes in to harass, intimidate, and interfere in a service, we can transmit the Holy Ghost through anointed gaze and command. Holy Ghost-filled leaders can look on people in an anointed gathering with the compassion of Jesus, and they will feel the love and presence of God come upon them.

The Catholic church has realized through exorcism that spiritual warfare involves strong commands. One of the commands they use includes the following: "I exorcize you, most unclean spirit, all spirits, every one of you. In the name of the Lord Jesus Christ, be uprooted and expelled from this creature of God. Go away, seducer. The Devil is your home. The Serpent is your dwelling. Be humiliated and cast down, for even though you have deceived men, you cannot make a mockery of God. He has prepared hell for you and your angels." (Catholic Encyclopedia, Exorcisms)

As a prayer of consecration, the priest prays for himself before he gets involved with the evil spirit, "All-powerful God, pardon all the sins of your unworthy servant. Give me comfort, faith, and power so that, armed with the power of Your holy strength, I can attack this cruel evil spirit in confidence and security."

The emphasis I am making is on strong words. We need to know that we are complete in God, who is the head over all principality and power. He has made us so that we can meet every occasion the Enemy might bring against us. Every siege that lies in wait to deceive and cripple the work of God is exposed.

CHAPTER 29
BIBLICAL STRUCTURE

One way to deal with the Devil is to build on the structure outlined in the Word of God. The Enemy cannot penetrate a fully armed house. The Holy Spirit wants to equip the body with every arsenal necessary for battle. Nothing shall be out of place—nothing broken, nothing missing. Everyone needs to know their gifts and callings. Although we strive for greater, we don't accept less. Jesus desires for the anointing for all believers to increase. Without structure, there is nothing to fill.

This is an essential prerequisite. Solomon had to build the temple to exact specifications before the glory of the Lord could fill it. (Tthe priests could not enter to minister until then.)

"Let all things be done decently and in order" could also mean that the biblical structure cannot be ignored. The Lord supplies the gifts. It is the duty of the leadership to extol His working in the body of the saints. Too many leaders think it is a one-man show.

A group of churches I was a part of once had a great visionary apostolic leader. People would say to you, "God loves you, and pastor G. has a wonderful plan for your life!" He exemplified servant leadership in preferring others and recognizing the incredible gifts that God had put into people.

Great leaders are not intimidated when God raises up others. In fact, they usually are mentoring one or two leaders at the same time to pass on the holy work so that it may grow and others may build more churches.

Once filled, believers will go out and speak the Word with boldness. When signs, wonders, miracles, healings, and anointed ministries begin to happen, it will not be necessary to make a plea for finances or people. They will come.

CHAPTER 30
SUMMARY, SIGNS, AND SYMPTOMS

Supernatural Burning

When Jesus walked with the two disciples on the road to Emmaus as they were discussing the Word, the disciples remarked later, "Did not our hearts burn within us?" (Luke 24:32). It is an interesting phenomenon that we can feel the Holy Spirit like heat inside of us.

I have felt supernatural heat and burning come all over my face, neck, and ears. I remember coming home after an intercessory prayer meeting one evening, and my wife remarked that my ears and cheeks were burning red. When we would sit together and discuss the Word, one lady would say often, "I feel a burning heat sensation coming up all over my back."

The anointing is tangible and wonderful. I have felt this warmth and burning sometimes lasting throughout services that followed the preservice prayer room experience. (A few of us would meet for prayer an hour before the scheduled evening service.)

At the Winnipeg Convention Centre in 1994, there was a large gathering of people coming together. The event was called Prairie Fire. As a casual observer, I went to check it out. There was a worship band playing for hours. This was just a long worship service, or so I thought. Then a speaker who was rather uncharismatic and not particularly interesting spoke for a while. There were many young people there. As they went up for prayer, it seemed that they were going up for more than prayer. It seemed they were going up for an experience with God.

I waited till almost the end, not particularly feeling anything, but I observed that lots of the young people were stumbling around. One young girl had to be held up and led by two others. It was like she was totally drunk.

Whatever they were experiencing, it was real. I was intrigued at what God was doing. I have come to appreciate the touch of God.

Supernatural Tranquility

We used to go to a Christian convention every summer in Edmonton. The kids had their own church lessons and fun events apart from the adults.

One day our oldest of four (who was then about eleven) said they had been "Benny-Hinned," which meant they had experienced being "slain in the spirit." (They were somewhat familiar with the phenomenon from watching Benny Hinn on Christian television.)

Our kids were very much at peace with the whole experience. Those days there was a kind of tranquility we experienced as a family. I remember starting out on our holiday. The kids would sit in the window and wave at all the traffic that we passed in our Sunliner motor home on the highway. Those were great memories.

One of our kids had a kidney disorder that sometimes made him very sick and gave him a bad fever. At that time we were not aware of what was causing it.

We had been to a healing night, and afterward we were all in our camper van. Jo-- was so sick, burning up with a fever. My wife and I both laid hands on him, and I prayed for him in his bed. She said, "I felt it leave." She was completely amazed. She had felt the fever go. He was totally fine the next morning. (In subsequent years he did have surgery to complete his healing.)

Deep Emotional Release

I am convinced a tangible experience with God can release one from emotional fears and trauma that may take years of counseling to get through. When the Lord sets you free, you can again take a deep breath, enjoy the life He has for you here on earth, and be renewed in your spirit and invigorated in your body.

People who have experienced some of these manifestations of the Spirit do not become terrorists. They are often filled with warm and wonderful feelings, restoring their souls and renewing their strength.

The Spirit without Measure

This is not something that just drops from the sky. Spiritual warfare must have a place in the body of Christ. Jesus has the Spirit without measure. We are His body, and we also have the potential for a much greater anointing than we can carry individually. We must begin to acknowledge the gifts of the Spirit in their administrations, their operations, and their manifestations.

An essential element is that we must deal with the Devil. This is done through regional declaration, proclamation, and intercession in the Spirit.

Worship and prophetic preaching are significant factors in building the gifts into the body. This takes careful work, allowing the master builder to work through us. We are His body. We must begin to acknowledge the supernatural ministry of intercession. As we release the Spirit of God in militant tongues of intercession, He will begin to flow like a mighty river in flood season.

Heaven is not holding back its glory. Thy will be done on earth, as it is in heaven. It is up to us to deal with the Devil.

CPSIA information can be obtained at www.ICGtesting.com
Printed in the USA
LVOW08s0354120814

398617LV00001B/9/P